CROWOOD SPORTS GUIDES
SNOOKER & BILLIARDS
TECHNIQUE•TACTICS•TRAINING

Clive Everton

The Crowood Press

First published in 1991 by
The Crowood Press Ltd
Ramsbury, Marlborough
Wiltshire SN8 2HR

www.crowood.com

This impression 2005

British Library Cataloguing in Publication Data

Everton, Clive
  Snooker and billiards: technique, tactics, training.– (Crowood sports guides series).
  I. Snooker. Billiards
  794.72

  ISBN 1 85223 480 6

Picture Credits
The line drawings were drawn by Taurus Graphics.
The photographs were supplied by Eric Whitehead.

Acknowledgements
Thanks to Jim Chambers. Jim is a professional snooker player and coach.

Throughout this book the pronouns 'he', 'him' and 'his' have been used inclusively and
are intended to apply to both males and females.

Typeset by Chippendale Type Ltd., Otley, West Yorkshire.
Printed in Singapore by Craft Print International Ltd.

CONTENTS

SNOOKER AND BILLIARDS

PREFACE

If you think that you cannot learn anything from books, then consider Steve Davis, who won six world titles in the eighties.

Steve Davis was perhaps not blessed with as much natural ability as Stephen Hendry or Jimmy White, both of whom seem to have been born with a cue in their hand, instead, he manufactured himself into the great player he has become.

In his teens, his bible was a book by Joe Davis, who won every world title on offer from 1927 to 1946. The book is long since out of print and some of its confident coaching assertions, accepted for years, have been superseded, but Steve derived an enormous amount of benefit from it, poring over it as he tried to acquire the technique which is the irreplaceable foundation of performance.

Instructional books have two functions: to tell you something you didn't know, or to remind you of something you may have forgotten or are no longer putting into practice. You won't improve simply by reading a book, but you might if you take up on the practice table the material within it. Many have.

Good luck and keep your chin down.

PART I
INTRODUCTION TO THE GAME

CHAPTER I

HISTORY

Billiards was the father of all billiard table games, but before Snooker came to be played, there already existed a number of other potting games. 'Pyramids' was played with the triangle of fifteen reds (with the apex red on what is now the pink spot), but no colours. It could be played by two or more players with an agreed stake per ball, or simply by two players – the first to pot eight reds being declared the winner.

A number of early pool games, so-called because the players were required to pool their bets in a kitty prior to commencement of play, also lent themselves to a flutter. 'Black Pool', for instance, was played, like Pyramids, with fifteen reds but also with the black placed either on the middle spot, or on what is now the black spot – this was then known as the billiards spot, i.e. the spot on which the red was placed in billiards. Anyone who potted the black extracted additional winnings from his opponents.

In 'Life Pool', each player adopted a different coloured ball and lost a 'life' (or monetary forfeit) when it was potted by an opponent. A player losing three 'lives' was 'dead' and the last player left 'alive' scooped the pool.

These were all popular games in 1875, not only in Britain but wherever there was a strong British influence. In the long hot summer of that year, in the Nilgiri Hills in Southern India, Field Marshal Sir Neville Bowles Chamberlain became aware of the boredom of the army officers who spent most of their days at the Ooty Club, Ootacamund. To relieve this, he decided to merge the elements of some of these existing games into a new game which came to be known as snooker.

The name 'snooker' originated from army slang. A 'snooker' (meaning the lowest of the low) was an expression attached to first year cadets at the Royal Military College, Woolwich. 'Snook' was also a derogatory Indian expression. When, therefore, whether by accident or design, a player so positioned the cue-ball that his opponent could not strike the ball 'on', he came to be referred to as a 'snooker'. From this came the verb 'to snooker', and hence the name of the game itself.

Chamberlain's original idea did not leave India until 1885 when John Roberts (junior) – not only the greatest player, but also the greatest entrepreneur of his day – met Chamberlain in Bangalore and brought the idea back to England. There, the John Roberts Billiard Supply Co began to commercialize the game with sales of snooker sets, which of course consisted of twenty-two balls and cost considerably more than a three-ball billiards set.

In contrast to billiards, in which good players could keep their opponents sitting out for long periods, snooker became popular as a more sociable type of game. Professionals were contemptuous of it but the game gained enough support among amateurs for the English Amateur Championship to be instituted in 1916.

A professional championship followed in 1927 through the personal initiative of Joe Davis, who duly won it and retained it until he retired from World Championship play in 1946, but snooker remained the poor relation to the Professional Billiards Championship until the mid-1930s.

The financial return rose gradually from the £6 10s. which Davis netted from his 1927 success and standards of play improved. In the early days, the general idea was to pot what was obviously on the table and then play a negative form of safety, but Davis himself was already evolving the sophisticated break-building techniques which now form part of the armoury of all leading players, and the tactical side of the game progressively developed its present complexity.

Fred Davis started to emerge as a threat to his elder brother and, in fact, only lost the 1940 world final 37–36. Horace Lindrum also gave the champion a good contest, 78–67, in 1946, the first world final from which the participants made any real money.

When Joe retired, Fred and the Scot Walter Donaldson dominated the scene until John Pulman became champion in

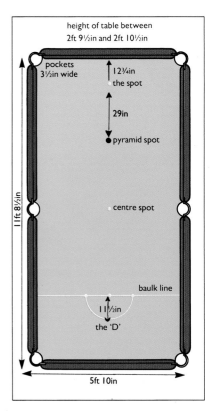

Playing surface dimensions.

height of table between
2ft 9½in and 2ft 10½in

pockets
3½in wide

12¾in
the spot

29in

pyramid spot

centre spot

11ft 8½in

baulk line

11½in

the 'D'

5ft 10in

1957 and retained the title until 1969. Unfortunately, and through no fault of Pulman, this era saw professional snooker almost disappear as a form of public entertainment and this remained the case until a new generation of professionals emerged in 1969.

In this year, John Spencer won the first of his three titles and the following year Ray Reardon won the first of his six. Alex Higgins won the title in 1972 and 1982.

Snooker's potential as a television sport was first glimpsed in 1969 with the launch of *Pot Black*, a weekly series on BBC 2, which also covered parts of major finals. Not until 1977, however, did the BBC decide to cover not only the final but the semi-finals of the 1977 World Championship, and only then did snooker attain a higher profile as a television sport.

The following year, the BBC instituted blanket coverage of the event from first ball to last, an innovation which established the sport with the viewing public, created a demand for more televised tournaments and thus shaped the season-long circuit which is currently in place.

Terry Griffiths won the world title in 1979, Cliff Thorburn in 1980 and Steve Davis in 1981, the first of six world championships he was to win in the eighties.

Dennis Taylor's victory over Steve Davis on the final black of the final frame of the 1985 world final attracted an amazing record BBC audience for a sporting event of 18.5M. Joe Johnson was the surprise winner of the 1986 championship, before the decade ended with a hat-trick of world titles for Davis. His winner's cheque in 1989 was for £105,000.

CHAPTER 2

THE GAME AND ITS OBJECTIVES

The game of snooker is played with a total of twenty-two coloured balls (fifteen reds, six colours and the white) which are positioned in exactly the same way at the beginning of every game (*see* Fig 1). The white, known as the cue-ball, is used alternately by both players and can be placed anywhere in the D for the opening stroke of the game, but from that point onwards it must be played from where it comes to rest.

The object of the game is to amass a greater number of points than your

opponent. Points are scored in two distinct ways, either by potting balls into the table's six pockets, or by penalties.

Each player must initially attempt to strike a red (value: 1). When the player succeeds in potting the red he must then play at a colour. The colours carry differing values: black 7, pink 6, blue 5, brown 4, green 3, yellow 2.

If the nominated colour is potted, it is not left in the pocket but replaced on its own spot before another red is attempted and so on, alternating reds and colours until all the reds have been potted.

Fig 1   The position of the balls at the start of every frame.

Fig 2   There is no need to nominate the blue, as it is obvious it is the colour that has been chosen.

Fig 3   When it is not obvious which colour has been selected, a player must state his choice clearly (in this case, brown, blue or pink).

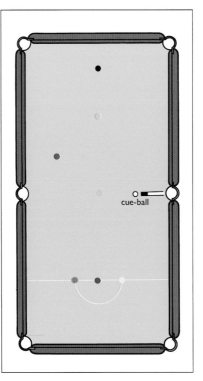

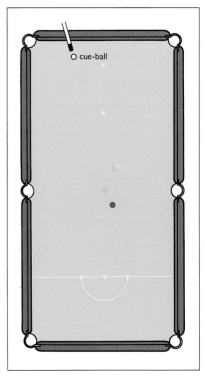

Fig 4 Jimmy White in action.

The colours are then taken in ascending numerical value, i.e. yellow first, black last, until only the cue-ball remains on the table.

This compilation of a sequence of pots is called a 'break'. A player forfeits his place at the table only when he has failed to pot the 'ball on' or has committed a foul in doing so.

Failure to strike a red when that is the ball on involves a penalty of four points (the minimum for any foul stroke) but the penalty points incurred increase to five, six or seven if, instead of a red, the cue-ball makes initial contact with the blue, pink or black.

An 'in-off', the second main type of foul shot, carries a four-point penalty – or more if the ball which the cue-ball initially struck before falling into a pocket is of a higher value. Following an in-off, the other player (the recipient of the penalty points) is allowed to place the cue-ball anywhere in the D.

The third common foul concerns the failure to hit a nominated colour, an offence which again involves a four-point penalty – or more if the ball involved is of a higher value. Therefore, if brown is nominated but black is struck the penalty is seven (the maximum). Likewise, if black is nominated but green is struck the penalty is also seven. Penalty points are not subtracted from the offender's score but instead are added to the score of his opponent.

The great majority of points are accrued by potting, but penalty points are not solely the result of inadvertency or bad luck. Skilfully laid snookers often force an opponent into committing errors and conceding penalties. A snooker occurs when the balls are so placed on the table that a player cannot strike the ball he is due to play without first hitting a cushion or making the cue-ball swerve. Crucially, the snooker very often has a tactical relevance to the game, above and beyond the four- to seven-point penalty gained or lost.

A Frame

The pyramid of reds is put into position prior to the commencement of every game with the aid of a triangular frame, usually made of wood or plastic. As a result of this, a single game of snooker has become known as a 'frame' and matches are made up of an agreed number of frames.

Amateur competitions usually consist of the best of three-, five- or seven-frame matches, while the final of the World Professional Championship is played over the best of thirty-five frames.

While this may seem a long distance, it is a veritable sprint when compared with the world finals of the immediate post-World War II years which were contested over 145 frames and took a fortnight to complete.

Number of Players

Snooker is predominantly a game which involves direct competition between two individuals, but – as in tennis – doubles or foursomes are accepted variations on the norm.

CHAPTER 3

THE RULES OF THE GAME AND THEIR APPLICATION

As in many other sports, such as golf and cricket, a workable understanding of the rules is essential for anyone who hopes to play snooker to a competitive standard. This knowledge does not come from reading the rule book cover-to-cover but largely from practical experience in playing the game.

Not every detail needs to be memorized (unless you aim to become an 'A' class referee), but in any number of situations a player can win or lose through his awareness of 'what is allowed' or 'what happens next'.

This section aims to explain the basic rules which can often confuse the novice and sometimes even the experienced exponent.

Foul Shots

Foul shots occur:

1. If a player's cue-tip strikes the cue-ball more than once in the same stroke and if cue-tip, cue-ball and object-ball make simultaneous contact. This is known as a push stroke.

> **RULES CHECK**
>
> A push-shot occurs when there is simultaneous contact between the cue-tip, the cue-ball and the object-ball.

Push strokes most commonly occur when cue-ball and object-ball are very close together. The nearer the two balls, the greater the likelihood of a push stroke. If the distance between the two balls is

under 1 in (2.5cm), an allowable shot is difficult unless the object-ball is struck thinly.

If the cue-ball comes to rest touching the object-ball, a player is obliged to play away without moving it. A good player often uses this to his advantage, for as the cue-ball can be played away without penalty, it does not have to make contact with any other ball. Playing a telling safety shot or snookering your opponent is thus often made simpler.

Fig 5   An attempted pot in the middle pocket: a position from which a push shot is common.

2. If a ball is forced off the table.
3. If a player plays a shot with both feet off the floor.
4. If a player strikes or touches a ball other than with the tip of the cue.
5. By causing the cue-ball to jump over any other ball.
6. By playing with the balls wrongly spotted.

As explained earlier, the six colours are re-spotted on their own designated spots after having been potted. If, however,

Fig 6   A simple two-cushion direct safety shot from a touching ball.

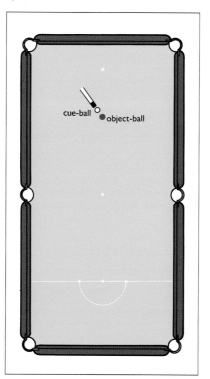

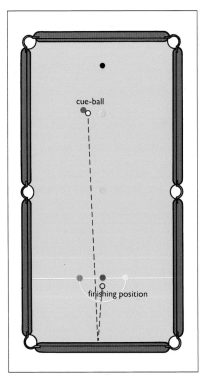

Fig 7   The laying of a snooker off a touching ball.

The ability to work out where colours will be positioned after they have been potted is of paramount importance when constructing a break. Lack of awareness leads directly to errors. On countless occasions, players can be heard to mutter, 'I forgot the brown had to go there', or, 'Why didn't I realize the black wouldn't spot'. Knowledge of the re-spotting mechanism reduces these frustrating *faux pas* to a minimum.

Free Ball and Play-Again Rulings

What Is a Free Ball?

If a player is snookered on the reds after a foul shot by his opponent he may nominate any coloured ball as a red. This is known as a 'free ball'. If it is potted, it counts one and a colour can then be nominated in the usual way.

If no red remains, a free ball is valued at the same number of points as the lowest value colour remaining and the colours are then taken in sequence.

For the purpose of this rule, a player is deemed to be snookered if he cannot directly hit both extremities of the object-ball.

Fig 8   With its own spot covered, the green is replaced on the spot of the highest value ball available, in this case the pink.

those spots are occupied or partially covered by other balls they are played on the highest available spot, e.g. if after potting the green that particular ball's spot is found to be unavailable and the pink, brown and yellow spots are free, the green would then be replaced on the pink spot.

Assuming that all the spots are covered, the colour is replaced nearest its own spot without touching another ball in a direct line between it and the nearest point on the top cushion.

The Relevance of a Free Ball

A free ball often turns a frame at top level as it frequently allows a player to start a sizeable break. It also provides a lifeline for the player who is seemingly in the hopeless position of needing several snookers to win.

Fig 9   Tony Meo placing the cue-ball in the 'D'.

For instance, if player A is forty-five points behind with just one red remaining (i.e. only thirty-five more points are available) he requires no less than three snookers and all the balls to win. However, if he lays one snooker which is missed by player B, thus leaving a free ball, a possible eight extra points are suddenly created (red 1, black 7) and player A is back in the reckoning. It is for this reason that professionals attempt to keep the last red on the table when they find themselves in the kind of predicament facing player A.

Etiquette

The origins of billiards as an indoor version of croquet; snooker's invention by British army officers in 1875 and the dinner jacket uniform of the professional player all suggest that snooker abides by certain codes of conduct which are almost sacred.

An appreciation of etiquette does not directly enhance performance, but the observance of the game's accepted code of conduct not only increases your enjoyment but ensures acceptability.

The Do's and Don'ts

1.   Two players usually decide who will break off by tossing a coin. Do not spin the coin over the table as the cloth could be damaged as a result.
2.   When your opponent is at the table, always try to keep noise to a minimum, never stand behind the pocket at which he is aiming, or anywhere else which could be distracting.
3.   In friendly frames and even in some low grade matches players do not have

referees. Therefore, when your opponent has potted a colour, re-spot it for him and call out his score at regular intervals during a break. If your opponent reciprocates, your concentration, when on a break, will be unimpeded.
4.   Always have good table manners. Play the game in the right spirit. Snooker professionals, like their golfing equivalents, maintain very high standards of sportsmanship: despite the huge amounts of money on offer, they retain enough integrity to call fouls on themselves which the referee may not have seen.

Playing Again

If your opponent makes a foul stroke which leaves you in an awkward position, you are entitled to ask that he play again. This rule, like the free ball rule, is aimed at preventing a player from gaining an advantage from making a foul stroke.

The most important consideration to

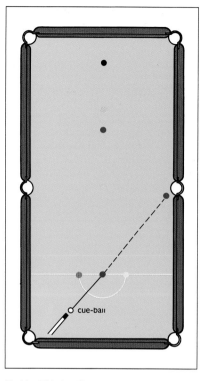

Fig 10   This shot illustrates how a free ball (in this case, the brown), is played onto a red in order to pot the red into the middle pocket.

bear in mind when deciding whether to make your opponent play again is whether or not by playing the shot yourself you can place him into even deeper trouble. If this is the case, play the shot yourself.

Other factors may also affect your decision and your thought processes can be illogical as a result of the pressure which the dilemma you face imposes on them.

If a pottable but risky shot has been left on, do you take the bull by the horns and attempt to pot it with the risk of losing the frame if you miss it; or do you elect to make your opponent play again, knowing that one good pot could lead to a frame-winning break?

An experienced professional would take the potting ability of his opponent, his own feelings about the shot and the match situation into account before making up his mind.

Before you make your opponent play again, always make doubly sure that you have not seen an easy pot or a set or plant (*see* Part 3, Chapter 10, page 76). Also be aware of left- or right-handedness. A shot may be particularly awkward for a right-handed player, but meat and drink to a left-hander and vice versa.

More Points on the Free Ball Ruling

In order to qualify for a free ball with reds on the table a player must be snookered on all of them. Therefore, if ten reds remain and following a foul stroke a player is snookered on nine of them – but is not obstructed from directly striking the tenth – a free ball cannot be awarded.

If reds remain and a free ball is given, it is within the rules to play the colour nominated as a red onto a 'real' red in order to pot it (*see* Fig 10).

However, if the nominated colour is missed and the cue-ball makes initial contact with a red, four penalty points will be incurred.

KIT CHECK

Always check whether a particular competition carries any specific dress stipulations or directives. The Billiards and Snooker Control Council, the governing body of the amateur game in Britain, have recently given referees the power to prevent players from competing in national events if they do not conform with the code. Anyone turning up in denims or training shoes faces disqualification.

How to Get Hold of a Rule Book

The full rules of snooker are complex and even the most experienced campaigners often do not know all of them. The official rule book available from the Billiards and Snooker Control Council (BSCC) will answer even the most obscure query.

CHAPTER 4

EQUIPMENT – THE TABLE AND ITS ACCESSORIES

A billiard table is to a snooker player what a cricket pitch is to a cricketer, or what a golf course is to a golfer. The major difference is that all tables are built to standard measurements, even though they may display subtle idiosyncrasies.

The Table

A snooker table has a level bed consisting of 2in (5cm) thick Italian or Portuguese slate, a green cloth surface and cloth-covered rubber cushions.

A full-size (championship) table measured from inside the cushion faces has a playing area of 11ft 8½in × 5ft 10in (3.6 × 1.8m). Pocket size is also uniform – it has to conform to templates issued by the BSCC. The rule on height says that a table can be between 2ft 9½in and 2ft 10in (85 and 86cm).

Tables of smaller size are also popular and constitute the ideal training ground for a young player not tall enough to play on a full-size table. These tables are usually 6ft × 3ft (182 × 91cm) or even 8ft × 4ft (243 × 121cm).

The Balls

As in golf, modern technology has allowed snooker balls to evolve into a vastly superior creation to the original balls made from wood or ivory. The most popular balls today, Super Crystalate, which are used in all major championships, are made from a resin compound and afford the modern player a greater chance to play a wide range of shots. Because they are more responsive to stun, side and screw shots the art of break-building and cue-ball control has been greatly enhanced. Each ball in a set is 2¹⁄₁₆in (5.2cm) in diameter and there should not be any more than 3g difference in their weight.

Rests

Often a player finds it difficult to reach a certain shot. Rests are the implements which allow him to do so. A standard rest is approximately 5ft (1.5m) long with an X-shaped head. This head acts as the player's hand on the table in that it holds the cue in position while the shot is being played. These rest-heads are made from plastic or steel. The steel ones are better because heavier and, therefore, less likely to move while the shot is being played.

Longer rests known as the 'half butt' and 'three-quarter butt' are also used when the length of the standard rest is not sufficient to reach a certain shot. Rests with elevated heads, known as 'spiders' help a player to execute a shot where intervening balls would obstruct the normal rest.

Equipment Required by the Individual – Cues, Chalk, Tips and Cue Cases

Cues

Compatibility with one particular cue is essential for anyone who wants to play snooker at a consistently high level. The

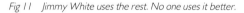

Fig 11   Jimmy White uses the rest. No one uses it better.

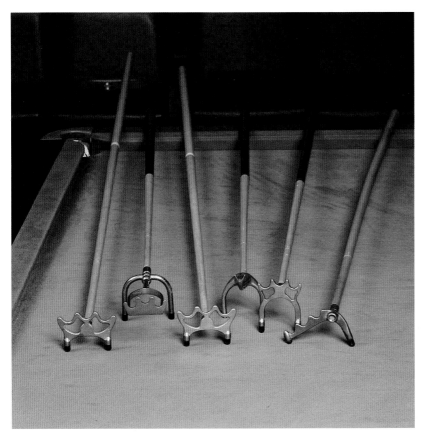

Fig 12   The range of rests available for the variety of awkward shots that crop up on occasions. The half and three-quarter butts are much longer than the normal rest.

Fig 13 (a) and (b)   Extensions on and off the cue. Their introduction has led to three-quarter butts (sometimes known as the 'fishing tackle') becoming virtually obsolete over the past few years.

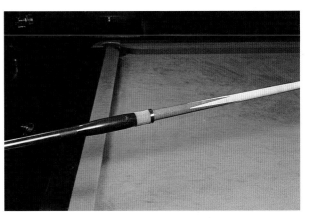

RULES CHECK

Although there is no upper limit on the length of a cue, it should not be less than 3ft (91cm) and should 'show no substantial departure from the traditional and generally accepted shape or form'.

top professionals may be the ultimate 'cueists', but if they were forced to wield a strange cue on each occasion they competed in a tournament, a rapid slide down the rankings would certainly ensue. Even for the lower grade amateur the importance of a successful and long-lasting partnership between player and cue cannot be over-emphasized.

KIT CHECK

Treat your cue with care. Regularly wipe it down with a damp rag and never leave it for long periods in excessive cold or heat. Too many players have taken their cue from its resting place – next to a radiator, or from a car – to find that it has become badly warped.

Only you are in a position to decide what is the perfect cue for yourself, as the optimum weight and length are determined by your own physical make-

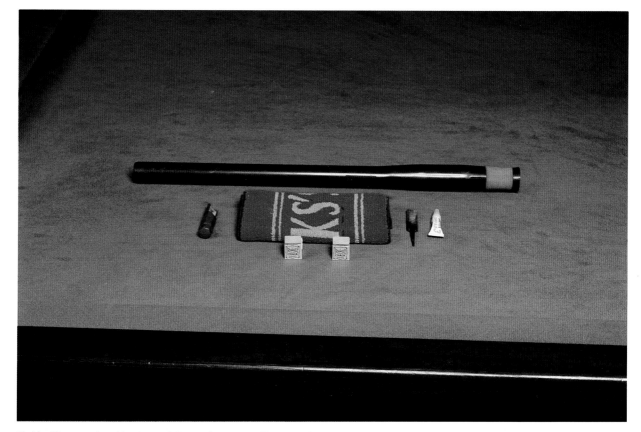

Fig 14   The extension with other useful items of equipment. Tip shaper, file, glue, chalk and bar towel.

up. The best cues are made of ash or maple; most weigh between 16–18oz (453–510g) and, as a guideline, it is generally agreed that the cue should reach around 2in (5cm) below shoulder level.

The 'feel' of a cue and the confidence it inspires in the player are also factors in the equation. Always remember that, within reason, there is no right and wrong in cue selection. A cue you feel happy with may not be to the liking of a practice partner, but that in itself does not mean it is the wrong cue for you.

Because cues can last, with proper care, a player's lifetime, their maintenance is obviously important. Never leave a cue where it will be subjected to extremes in temperature, e.g. next to a radiator, or in a car during winter. Likewise, do not leave

---

RULES CHECK

The rules of snooker state that a player's cue must be at least 3ft (91cm) long and must ' . . . conform to the accepted shape and design'; but until a professional called Alec Brown was involved in a bizarre incident in 1938, no such stipulation existed.

With the cue-ball marooned in the pack of reds, Brown produced a tiny ebony cue from his pocket and proceeded to play the shot. When his opponent protested, the referee decided that the use of the miniature cue was outside the spirit, if not the letter, of the rule. It was then obvious that a new rule was needed to fill the loophole that Brown had attempted to exploit.

---

it propped up against a wall as this leads to the cue becoming warped. Always guard against theft, for if your cue is lost it is highly probable that your game will be adversely affected.

KIT CHECK

Always make doubly sure that your chalk, which should be green, is neither damp nor flaky. If it is, your chances of a miscue are much greater.

Over the past ten years the two-piece cue has come more and more into vogue. Its obvious advantage over a one-piece is that it is more easily transportable and, as it has become more refined, top players such as Steve Davis and Jimmy White have felt sufficiently confident in their performance to use one.

In fact, Davis decided to have his trusty one-piece cue converted into a two-piece after suffering a series of cue problems at the start of the 1987/1988 season. The delicate operation was performed in October 1987. Afterwards, Davis said: 'It's a better cue than it was before. I'm able to do a lot more with it, particularly on power shots.'

Tips, Chalk and Cue Cases

Elk Master and Blue Diamond are considered to be the best tips available today. When put in place, a tip should always be gently domed with a file (another useful piece of equipment) in order to attain maximum benefit. In terms of texture, there is a fine dividing line between firmness and hardness. A really hard tip tends to skid off the ball, while soft tips, with their 'spongy' feel, make all forms of spin shots more difficult to perform.

The tip must always be chalked at regular intervals throughout a frame to keep miscues, often costly, to a minimum.

National Tournament and Triangle chalks, both of which are manufactured in the US, are the most popular. The green-coloured variety is most widely used as it does not stick to the cue-ball unless damp. The gimmicky red chalk which is on the market should be avoided, as it often leaves marks on a table's surface which cannot be brushed out.

Good, solid cue-cases may seem expensive, but one which protects the cue properly when it is not being used is a good investment.

> **KIT CHECK**
>
> If you practise a lot, you will find that the constant pulling out and replacing of the chalk in your pocket will ruin your trousers. This damage can be avoided by using a magnetic cue-grip – an innovation in the accessories market – or a pouch (like Willie Thorne).

Guidelines on Clothing

Only the top professionals wear a uniform, i.e. a dress suit with a shirt and tie, when they are competing in a tournament. Otherwise, no specific clothing requirements exist in snooker. Most clubs, however, discourage scruffy

> **KIT CHECK**
>
> If you reach the standard where the purchase of a dress suit is a must, you should instruct your tailor that the trousers must be high-waisted and the waist coat low-cut. This is to prevent unsightly gaps between the two when you are down on a shot.

attire and the amateur sport's governing body, the BSCC, have protected dress standards by putting a ban on players wearing denims or training shoes in the English Amateur Championship.

From a practical point of view, it is obvious that slippery footwear can cause a player to experience problems with his stance – baggy sleeves lead to foul shots being committed as a player leaning over a ball inadvertently touches a red.

Take pride in your appearance, as the 'good feeling' this will give you can be just the psychological edge needed to produce a satisfying performance.

PART 2

SKILLS
AND
TECHNIQUES

CHAPTER 5

THE GRIP

Depending on his individual physical characteristics, every player will exhibit a slightly different stance and overall cue action. This also applies to the grip. Even the top professionals do not all grip the cue in the same manner.

However, their differing grips do have one vital thing in common. They all allow the cue to flow up to and through the cue-ball in a straight line.

Physical idiosyncrasies mean that it is impossible to put forward the concept of a uniform grip which would work equally effectively for all players. What is right for one player is wrong for another and vice versa. For instance, if your wrist tends to turn to the left, causing your elbow to jutt out from the body, your cue will be held in the palm of your hand. Conversely, if the wrist is naturally inclined to turn your hand to the right, the grip goes more into the fingertips.

Fig 15 All four fingers should be wrapped around the butt at the start of a stroke.

The cue should always be held a few inches from the butt with the four fingers giving varying degrees of support to keep it horizontal when playing a shot. A medium-strength overall grip is also important if it is to be effective. The very light, loose grips used by billiard players of old, make stun and screw shots extremely difficult to execute. Holding the cue too fiercely – a much more common failing nowadays – produces tension in the cue-arm, which results in a loss of fluency and a tendency for the cue not to go right through the cue-ball.

Fig 16 Hold the cue 3 or 4in (7 or 10cm) from the butt.

Fig 17 Front view of the grip, showing firmness in the wrist.

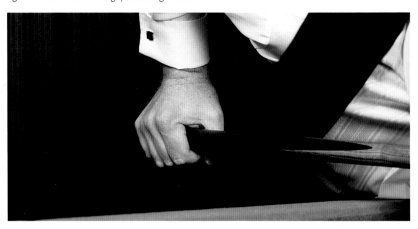

Fig 18 (a), (b) and (c)   Side and rear views of third and fourth fingers being relaxed on the backswing.

By far the most common fault committed by a novice is that he grips the cue too fiercely. Given that a 'scooping' cue action leads to frequent miscues, it becomes clear·that keeping the cue as horizontal as possible when playing the shot is vitally important. If the grip is too tight this will be impossible to achieve (except for a short, slow shot) because you will automatically raise the butt end of the cue above the horizontal as the cue swings back.

KEY POINT

Grip: a fine dividing line exists between holding the cue too fiercely or too lightly. It is hard to generate power if the grip is weak, but a tight grip causes unwanted tension in the cue arm.

In order to retain the strength of grip essential for the power shots which are such an integral part of the modern game – and to keep the cue horizontal at the same time – the grip of the second and

Fig 19   Ray Reardon demonstrates the use of the rest.

third fingers should be slightly eased on the backswing. Then, as the cue is pushed forward towards the cue-ball, the original grip should be re-applied to produce the power needed. The grip of the thumb and first finger should not alter in strength throughout the shot.

The little finger (fourth finger) of your grip hand should be totally relaxed and could even be lifted off the cue altogether if you so wished. This is because the strength of the little finger should have a negligible significance on the shot. John Parrott and Jimmy White – the two players on the circuit most renowned for their prodigious cue-power – adopt what is basically a three-finger grip.

Bridge

When a basic efficient grip has been developed, the next step is to be able to form a bridge with the other hand. If you imagine the overall stance as a tripod, then the function of the bridge-hand is to act as the front leg. Its role is as in the tripod: to hold the stance firm. A good bridge does not guarantee success, but is a pre-requisite for it.

All advanced players have a bridge-hand which grips the cloth firmly while

KEY POINT

Bridge: the thumb and fingers of the bridge-hand play a vital role. Fingers that grip the cloth give the bridge stability. A correctly cocked thumb promotes accurate ball striking.

RULES CHECK

Always make sure when bridging or leaning over an intervening ball that no part of your anatomy or clothing is touching the ball.

Fig 20   Jimmy White. Note his concentration.

also providing a channel between thumb and forefinger. This channel's job is to maintain the cue on a straight line as it is pushed towards the cue-ball.

Making a bridge is simple enough. Place the bridge-hand flat on the surface of the table, draw up all the fingers in a crab-like fashion, then cock the thumb high in order to form a V-shaped channel between the thumb and the top knuckle of the forefinger. The bridge should then be resting on its heel: the underpart of the thumb and the fingertips. The optimum distance between the bridge-hand and the cue-ball varies from shot to shot.

The distance between the bridge-hand and the white depends on the type of shot being attempted. If, for instance, you are rolling the cue-ball up behind a colour in order to lay a snooker, the space between bridge-hand and cue-ball will not be as great as that for a forcing shot.

The correct formation of the V-shaped channel is essential if consistently straight cueing is to be attained. If it is too wide, the cue will be free to wobble from side to side. This will cause the cue to deviate

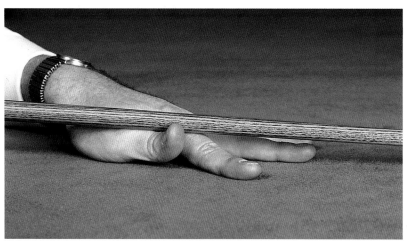

Fig 21   Side view of the bridge – the stability of the bridge is increased by the fingertips gripping the cloth.

Fig 22   Front view of the bridge. This clearly shows how the thumb should be cocked: the channel between thumb and forefinger this produces allows the cue to run through smoothly without wobbling from side to side.

TOMMY POSTLETHWAITE

Tommy Postlethwaite was one player who proved to be an exception to the rule. Despite not being able to form a channel between his thumb and forefinger, he reached the final of the English Amateur Championship in 1949.

Postlethwaite, a sheet metal worker from Wolverhampton, was forced to bridge between his forefinger and middle fingers after severing thumb tendons when he was twenty. He overcame the handicap by making a few adjustments and was one of Britain's leading amateurs throughout the forties and fifties.

Fig 23   Notice how widely the fingers are spread.

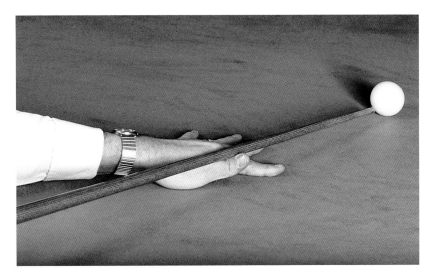

Fig 24   The optimum distance between the cue-ball and the bridge-hand is anything between 6 and 8in (13 and 20cm).

from a straight line, with the undesirable effect of placing unintentional side-spin on the cue-ball.

Given that the bridge acts as the front leg of a tripod, it needs to be immovable. This is achieved by gripping the cloth fiercely with the pads of the fingers, especially the forefingers. Fred Davis, eight times World Champion from 1948 to 1956 was noted for this kind of finger grip. Indeed, he was often criticized for leaving marks on the cloth which were the direct consequence of the pressure he put on his fingertips. Davis had a sensible reason for doing this. He knew that a firm bridge helps all but the cue-arm stay still when a shot is being played, and therefore aids accuracy of strike.

Stance

For any player to have a solid stance he must be well-balanced. If that is the case and the stance achieves its ultimate objective of allowing the player to cue in a straight line, it is satisfactory.

As with the grip, all members of the professional ranks do not possess identical stances, but even with their differences their own individual stances promote the same high level of accuracy.

Nevertheless, all effective stances do share some common features. The back leg (right, if right-handed) should be braced and you should lean forward, putting your weight on the front leg. This leg should be bent so that you move into the shot. By adopting this method, your weight distribution means that the body is less likely to move when you swing your

cue-arm. Steve Davis maintains that if someone attempted to knock him off balance once he had taken his snooker stance, he could move only forward.

Forming a stance in-line with the shot is relatively easy if a simple procedure is followed. When you get down to play, put your cue on a straight line to the shot, then move your body to the cue.

Always bear in mind that for a stance to be successful it must work for *you*. If you consciously try to keep in a certain position because you perceive it to be the 'right' way to play (but feel uncomfortable as a result), confidence, timing and rhythm will almost certainly disappear. Players are not robots, so it is impossible to become a carbon copy of your favourite player. By all means study the stances of the experts, even draw benefit from imitating their strengths, but never compromise your own natural style.

Fig 25   Steve Davis's cue goes right through the middle of the cue-ball.

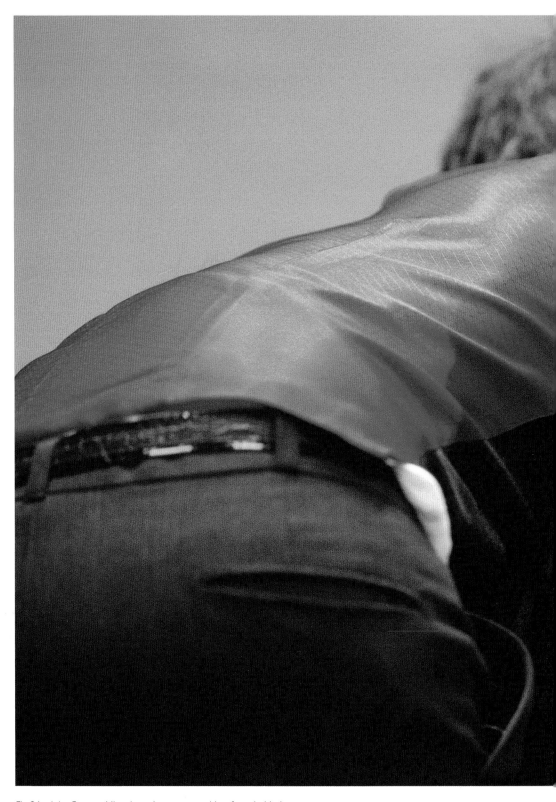

Fig 26   John Parrott. His grip and cue-arm position from behind.

Fig 27   Back view of the stance, showing the distance the feet should be apart.

Fig 28   Side view of the stance – the back leg is braced, while the slightly bent front leg is taking the majority of Jim's body-weight.

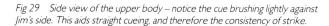

Fig 29   Side view of the upper body – notice the cue brushing lightly against Jim's side. This aids straight cueing, and therefore the consistency of strike.

Sighting the Shot

As snooker is a game which allows little margin for error, correct sighting is vitally important. Your grip, bridge and stance may allow the cue's delivery to be arrow-straight, but this is rendered useless if your alignment leads to the wrong spot on the object-ball being aimed at. For many years it was advocated that the cue should brush the chin directly below the nose so that both eyes could concentrate on the shot. However, in recent times, this theory has been largely discredited.

The method is ideal if your eyes are of equal strength, but it falls down if – as is

Fig 30 (a) and (b)　Rear view of Jim, displaying a stance where the feet are too wide apart and much too close together.

KEY POINT

Sighting: the best cue action in the world is completely useless if it belongs to a blind man. Always remember the importance of running the cue under the 'master eye' if you have one.

often the case – one of your eyes is stronger than the other. The dominant eye is called 'the master eye'. Both Joe Davis and former World Professional Billiards Champion Rex Williams are left-eyed, while John Virgo sights under his right eye. If you do have a 'master eye', your sighting will be at its most accurate if the cue is run directly under that eye.

EYE TEST

If doubts are now beginning to form in your mind as to which, if either, is your 'master eye', a simple test will provide the answer.

Place a piece of chalk at one end of the table, then stand directly in front of it at the other. Point your forefinger at the chalk, first with both eyes open, then with your right eye closed. If your finger is still pointing at the chalk, you are left-handed. If this is the case, when you re-open your right eye and close the left, the finger will be pointing to the left of the chalk. If you are even-sighted and have no dominant eye, like Stephen Hendry, the finger will move slightly to the right or left, whichever eye you shut.

Always remember that you should be looking at the spot on the object-ball for which you are aiming at the instant the shot is played. Taking the eyes off the object-ball a split second before the shot has been executed is a frequent mistake amongst novices. While it is tempting to look up to see if a particular ball has been potted, or if the cue-ball has gained its intended position, a player should not be over-eager. As in golf, head up (and consequently eyes away from the target) is an elementary failing. All top players keep head and upper body as still as possible until the shot has been played.

Fig 31　Sighting the shot – Jim is an even-sighted player; he has no 'master eye'. The cue runs directly beneath his chin.

Fig 32　Notice the elbow of Jim's cue arm is exactly in-line with the top of his head, which, in turn, is in-line with the two balls and the pocket.

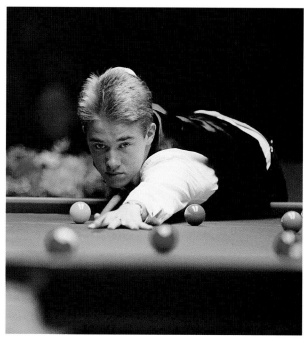

Fig 34   Sighting the shot – Stephen Hendry (even-sighted).

Fig 35   John Virgo – right-eyed.

Fig 33   Back view of this perfect alignment.

Fig 36   Rex Williams – left-eyed.

Fig 37   Tony Meo sizing up all the angles before attempting to escape from a snooker.

Fig 38   The cue action. The hinge opens at the end of the backswing.   Fig 39   Side view.

Cue Action

With alignment and sighting correct, only one more attribute is required to make the cue-ball go to the desired spot: a consistently straight delivery – a dependable cue action.

If it is possible to drawn an analogy, the perfect cue action performs like a hinge. This hinge opens as the cue is pulled back and closes when the cue is pushed forward towards the cue-ball. This cue arm movement should be the only moving part of your body. If shoulders or any other part of the upper body come into play, there is a tendency for the head to come up off the shot with disastrous results. Alex Higgins is prone to a massive amount of body movement when playing power shots. As his co-ordination has worsened with age, he is potting a smaller and smaller percentage of these types of shot.

When you are in the address position before the shot, take a number of rhythmical preliminary short strokes which

Fig 42   The movement of the cue required in relation to the cue-ball on the backswing.

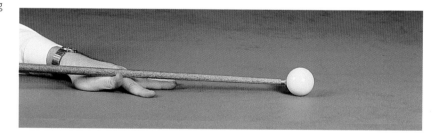

Fig 43   Contact.

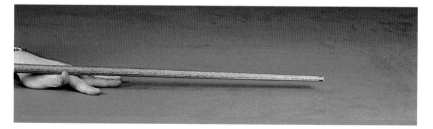

Fig 44   Follow-through.

KEY POINT

Cue action: think of yourself as a piece of machinery: the movement of the forearm should be the only working cog as the shot is played.

Fig 40   *The follow-through.*

Fig 41   *The hinge closes at the end of the follow-through (side).*

obviously should not touch the cue-ball. These 'addresses' do the same job as 'waggles' of the club by a golfer, in that they serve to heighten your concentration and prepare you for the shot ahead.

Often, a beginner takes the cue back in short disjointed jerks, or pulls the cue back far too much. In fact, the cue should be brought back smoothly and at an even pace. Then it should be held at the top of the backswing for a fraction of a second before coming forward, striking through the cue-ball for a few inches (the follow-through) prior to stopping in the same groove.

Even when you have developed a reasonable cue action, it does no harm to your game to make any minor technical alterations that are felt necessary. The smallest change can work wonders and give you a new-found confidence. Nevertheless, beware of constant tinkering. If you are satisfied with a particular feature of your cue action, do not experiment solely for change's sake. Consistency is a crucial ally for any snooker player. Thoughtless tinkering can cause it to disappear.

Supplementary Bridges

Billiards and snooker would be far easier games if players could always make the perfect bridge. However, because of the cushions – and sometimes the position of the balls in relation to the cue-ball – this is impossible. There are, therefore, a number of bridges which need to be learnt if a player is to cope with all situations.

One of the trickiest of positions is when playing from tight under a cushion. In his instructional book entitled *Complete Snooker*, Joe Davis said that this type of shot is best played with the fingers flat on the cushion rail. Nowadays, however, most top players play with the wrist dropped below the level of the cushion and with the bridge-hand slightly raised.

The disadvantage of this is that you are striking downwards at the cue-ball, thus increasing the possibility of imparting

Fig 45   *Supplementary bridges – the 'cushion bridge'. Fingers pressed against wooden cushion rail to play cue-ball tucked tight under cushion.*

Fig 46   'Looped' bridge – suitable for playing a ball which lies some inches away from the cushion, but in such a position that the normal bridge is impossible.

unintentional side onto it. You can make this cushion bridge reasonably steady by pressing down on the pads of the fingers, but there is bound to be a certain degree of unsteadiness. Therefore, do not try anything too difficult as regards position when you have to make this bridge and be especially reluctant to employ forcing shots. Concentrate even more than usual on keeping still and cut down your backswing, keeping the stroke as brief and as simple as possible.

Bridging over a ball brings out most of the problems that are encountered in playing from under, or near to, a cushion. Spread the fingers widely, then lean down on them to give the bridge stability. When the intervening ball between the bridge and cue-ball is very close, the bridge will need to be almost vertical, but as this space increases to a few inches, neither the bridge-hand nor the cue needs to be raised so high.

As when under the cushion, the most

prudent policy, even for the best players, is to keep the shot simple. The advantage of possessing long fingers in this type of position is considerable, as they make it easier to get the necessary elevation of the bridge so that the cue can strike downwards at the small part of the ball that is available to be hit. The bridge is placed as near as possible to the intervening ball and the cue, as it strikes downwards, should miss the intervening ball by the smallest possible margin.

Fig 47 (a) and (b)   Side and front view of Jim's excellently elevated high bridge for playing shots over intervening balls. Long fingers obviously help, but short fingers can gain elevation if the middle two fingers are kept as upright as possible.

Fig 48   A high, two-fingered bridge from Dennis Taylor.

Fig 49 (a) and (b)   Terry Griffiths bridging over an intervening ball. Note the wide-spread fingers and leant-down position for increased stability.

Supplementary Stances

Provided that one foot remains touching the floor until the shot is completed, certain shots which would otherwise require the rest can be made with the orthodox bridge, by lifting one leg off the ground, sometimes on to the cushion rail.

> **RULES CHECK**
>
> A striker must be touching the ground with at least one foot as the stroke is being played.

When the cue-ball is on the other side of the table, you often see players standing

Fig 50   A supplementary stance – using the table to your advantage.

Fig 51   By placing either the left or right leg on a particular cushion rail, you can extend your reach and sometimes avoid having to use the rest.

stork-like on their front leg (the left, if they are right-handed) with the right leg waving in the air. It is hard to stay completely steady on the shot if you stand like this and it is therefore preferable, when possible, to place your back leg on the table, letting it take your weight, while the front leg is touching the floor. This more stable, solid stance enables you to get into a more horizontal position for the shot, while the stork-like stance merely leaves you looking downwards into the bed of the table rather than along the line of the shot.

CHAPTER 6

STUN, SCREW AND SIDE

Once the mechanics of grip, stance and plain ball-striking have been mastered, there are certain basic skills which have to be acquired, namely side, screw and stun.

At the turn of the century, when snooker was still in its embryonic stage and standing in the shadow of billiards as a popular attraction, the game was played in a much less cultured way than today. Positional play was very basic until the arrival in the twenties of the far-sighted Joe Davis who began to realize than an ability to play stun, screw and side shots would give him a considerable advantage over his contemporaries. By trial and error in long solo practice sessions, Davis developed these skills. The result was akin to the opening of a Pandora's Box of snooker skills, as more and more players began to employ these 'advanced shots' in their repertoire. Century breaks, rather than being treated as a miracle, now became an accepted part of the game and, today, side, stun and screw shots are an integral feature of every frame.

Side

Side is imparted by the tip of the cue striking either to the left or right of the centre of the cue-ball. Fig 53 shows what happens when right-hand side is used. First the cue-ball pushes out slightly to the left and then curls back with the spin. When the cue-ball strikes a cushion, the spin is fully activated so that it rebounds sharply to the right. Due to the scale of the diagram, this curve has been exaggerated.

Fig 55 shows how the ball spins differently when it is travelling down the table (i.e. towards the baulk). Because the ball is running against the nap of the cloth, the initial thrust to the left – which occurs when right-hand side is imparted – is maintained instead of the ball spinning to the right, though, of course, the ball still spins to the right after hitting a cushion.

The number of instances in which side (right- or left-hand) may be used is infinitely varied, but for the purposes of definition you should know the difference between 'running side' and 'check side'.

Fig 52   Here, Jim shows a plain-ball shot. He has hit the ball in the centre, causing no spin to be imparted.

Fig 53   Path of the cue-ball when hit with right-hand (running) side.

Fig 54   Here, extreme right-hand side-spin will be achieved.

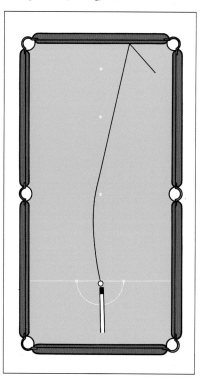

Running side is the type of spin shown in Fig 53: right-hand side has been used to widen the angle at which the cue-ball leaves the cushion and has also, incidentally, increased the distance the cue-ball will run.

Check side does the opposite: right-hand side narrows the angle at which the cue-ball leaves the cushion and reduces the run of the cue-ball.

How can right-hand side be 'running' in one position and 'check' in another? In Fig 53, the cue-ball contacts the cushion and the 'running' side acts to exaggerate its natural tendency to move to the right. In Fig 56, the cue-ball contacts the left of the object-ball and, of course, still goes on the left, but in this case the right-hand side of the cue-ball fights this natural tendency and the cue-ball 'checks' as the spin bites into the cushion.

There is one very important aspect of cueing to remember when using side of any description: the cue should go through

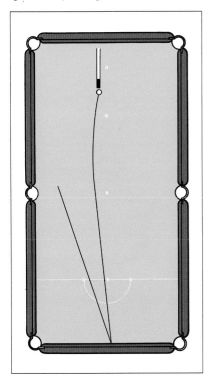

Fig 55   Path of the cue-ball when hit against the nap with right-hand side.

---

the cue-ball rather than catch it a glancing blow. In other words, do not address the cue-ball in the centre and then hit it on one side or another, but address it at the point you intend to hit and strike straight through it. The point to remember is that side is best applied by hitting through the ball in its 'thick part'. If the cue hits either of the cue-ball's extreme edges, not so much side will be imparted and the danger of a 'miscue' increases. It is the act of cueing through the ball, not just brushing its edge, that creates side-spin.

Running and check side can also

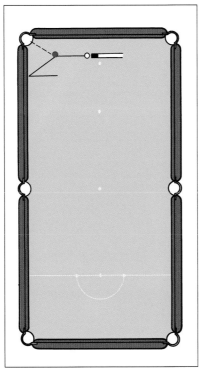

Fig 56   This illustrates how check side narrows the angle at which the cue-ball leaves the cushion.

---

operate off balls as well as cushions, though the effect is not as pronounced. If (as in Fig 56) you are attempting to pot the red with check side, you must aim to hit the red 'thinner', as check-side straightens the object-ball up after it has made contact with the cue-ball. Conversely, if the shot was being played with 'running' side, the object-ball would have to be hit thicker than if the shot was being played with no side.

Side is vital in positional play but its application to the cue-ball, even by the most experienced player, can be fraught with danger. Steve Davis, a player renowned for his robot-like cue action, plays only with side when there is no other alternative. Novices be warned – do not walk before you can run.

Fig 57   The right and wrong way to impart side-spin. Do not place the bridge-hand in a position to strike the middle of the cue-ball and then strike across it, as the cue on the left is doing. It is vital, when playing with side, to strike through the cue-ball in a straight line.

Fig 58   Dennis Taylor gets his cue-arm high to swerve the cue-ball.

Screw

Most novices regard screw shots, i.e. those shots with backspin, as akin to magic, when in reality they are quite simple.

When applying screw, lower the bridge slightly to maintain the horizontal angle at which the tip strikes the cue-ball and always hit cleanly through the ball. Do not jab at the cue-ball or strike too low. Follow through so that you can 'feel' the cue-ball on the tip of your cue. The most common mistake made by beginners is to strike down into the cue-ball instead of dropping the bridge to keep the cue horizontal.

Place a ball on the 'blue spot' and put the cue-ball approximately 9in (20cm) away, just off straight, between it and a middle pocket. Strike the cue-ball below centre at medium pace and follow the procedure set out above.

If you do all these things correctly, the cue-ball will spin back in the general direction of the other middle pocket, depending on the speed of the shot and the spin imparted. It was once advocated that this shot should be set up straight, but the fault in this theory is that with the cue-ball spinning back at the player's tip he has to move sharply to avoid it. A movement of this nature, on this particular type of shot, is not wanted.

When the cue-ball is struck below centre, it skids backwards towards the object-ball, rather than keeping going over and over like a wheel. On impact with the object-ball, this reverse spin comes into effect and the cue-ball recoils.

Often players put too much effort into screw shots, getting their arm tense, moving their upper body and slamming at the ball, instead of cueing smoothly as you would with an ordinary plain-ball shot. With practice you should find that you are able to control almost to the inch how far you bring the cue-ball back.

Screw shots with the object-ball more than 9in (20cm) away are more difficult because the backspin gradually evaporates the further the cue-ball has to travel before contacting the object-ball.

DEEP SCREW

John Spencer was widely regarded as one of the best 'deep screw' exponents of the late sixties and seventies and it was the perfect execution of one of these difficult shots that proved the turning point in the 1970 World Professional Championship final in which Spencer captured the second of his three world titles.

Fig 63 (see page 50) illustrates one shot from his 42–31 victory over Australian Warren Simpson, which Simpson himself described as 'impossible'. With no less than 8ft (2.40m) between cue-ball and object-ball, Spencer was aiming to screw back some 3ft (90cm) for the blue or one of the baulk colours, but with perfect timing allied to tremendous cue-power, he caused the cue-ball to screw back onto the side then bottom cushions, a total distance of approximately 12ft (3.65m). Not surprisingly, this prodigious feat earned him a three-minute ovation from the audience.

Fig 59   The whole bridge must be lowered for a screw shot, in order that the cue is kept as parallel as possible to the cloth.

Fig 60   Do not hit down on the cue-ball as many players mistakenly do. You will only get a minimum of back-spin, your accuracy will be reduced and there is a risk of damage to the table.

Fig 61   When applying top-spin, the opposite procedure to playing a screw shot is adopted. The bridge is raised slightly, so that even though the cue is striking the top of the white, it is still almost horizontal to the playing surface.

Fig 62   Hitting down into the white when trying to play with top-spin causes the 'massé' effect. The white swerves and throws off its intended line.

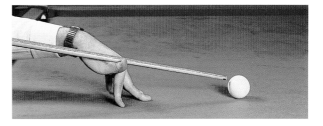

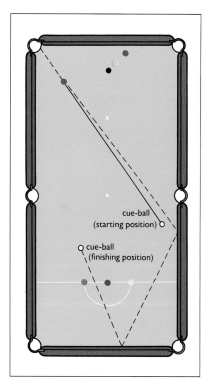

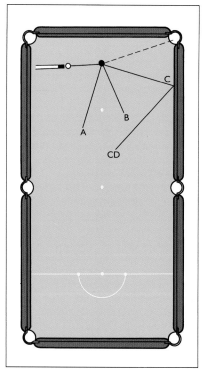

Fig 63   John Spencer's incredible deep screw shot in the 1970 World Championship Final.

Fig 64   Some of the positions. It is possible to place the cue-ball after this pot.

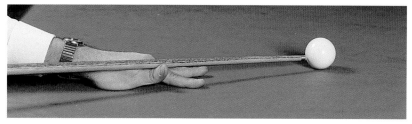

Fig 65   If the cue- and object-balls are close together, the stun effect can be attained by striking the white just below centre. The further the balls are apart, the lower on the cue-ball the player has to strike.

Therefore, the further the object-ball is from the cue-ball, the more power is needed and the more important it is to strike as low as possible without miscueing.

Stun

Stun can mean two things:

1.   With a straight shot it means stopping the cue-ball dead on impact.
2.   With a shot at an angle it means widening the angle at which the cue-ball leaves the object-ball.

When the cue-ball and the object-ball are close together, the cue-ball needs only to be struck very slightly below centre to stop it dead. When the balls are further apart, you need to strike much lower.

As soon as you get beyond the most elementary level of play, you will realize that positional play is what snooker is all about. The significance of Fig 64, therefore, is to show the range of positions which are open to a player who has a good command of the basic skills. The range includes anywhere on line A (full screw), line B (stun), line C (plain ball run through) and line D (run through with right-hand side).

As you progress and improve, you will develop the touch and control necessary to manoeuvre the cue-ball into the positions you want.

CHAPTER 7

THE THEORY AND PRACTICE OF POTTING

Consistent potting is without any doubt the most important facet of snooker. Lengthy breaks are almost impossible to compile if you cannot pot reasonably well and frames are difficult to win without them. Accurate positional play complements good potting and makes breaks easier to put together, but a beginner should not compromise his potting by attempting complicated cue-ball control. Take it one step at a time, master the art of potting before turning your attentions to advanced positional play.

How to Pot

With any pot, the object-ball is sent towards the pocket by the cue-ball striking it in a certain place. Before each shot, Steve Davis imagines the cue-ball covering the object-ball at the split-second contact between the two is made.

Dead-straight shots require the whole of the cue-ball to cover the object-ball at the moment of impact. This is called a full-ball contact.

However, only a small percentage of

shots are straight. Most pots can be achieved only if the cue-ball sends the object-ball off at a particular angle. Sometimes, the cue-ball will have to cover half of the object-ball so a half-ball contact is needed. If, because of poor cueing or faulty estimation of the type of contact required, the white strikes the object-ball closer to three-quarter ball (too full) the shot will be missed because the pink will have been hit too thickly (undercut). Conversely, if the cue-ball hits the object-ball nearer quarter-ball (overcut) the pot

Fig 66   Full-ball pot. The whole of the cue-ball is required to cover the object-ball at the moment of impact.

Fig 67   The off-straight pot which requires ¾ of the white to cover the object-ball at the moment of impact.

Fig 68   Half-ball contact.

Fig 69 Potting at a stretch with a raised bridge – Neal Foulds.

will again go astray, but on the opposite side of the pocket.

Potting is a matter of individual judgement. With little experience a novice may possess a sound cue-action, but will not be able to pot well. This is because he does not know the correct place to aim for on the object-ball.

STAR TIP

Even the greatest players miss pots. No one is infallible – if we were, snooker would cease to be a game.
(Dennis Taylor, *Play Snooker*)

As you improve and gain more knowledge, the instances where a pot is missed because of an incorrect angle assessment become less frequent. Experienced players automatically know the target on the object-ball and pot it.

Fig 70   Thin snick.

Fig 71   Desired half-ball contact is attained and the object-ball is potted.

Fig 72   The object-ball is undercut – hit too thickly – and the pot is missed.

Fig 73   The object-ball is overcut – hit too thinly – and the pot is missed.

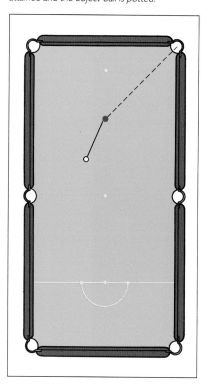

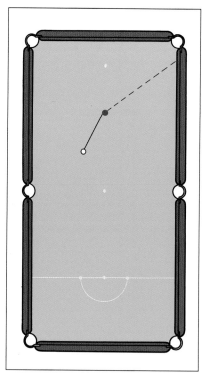

This is why practice is so vitally important for 'keeping your eye in'.

Given that experienced players know where to hit the object-ball, the only other reason why a pot is missed must be a deficiency in the cue action. In other words the aim can be spot-on, but if the cue-ball does not go in the intended direction, the player concerned will fail on the pot.

Frank Callan, probably the world's foremost expert on technique, believes that a player can quickly discover whether he is cueing straight by checking the direction of the cue against the baulk line.

Just cue along the baulk line at an imaginary cue-ball. If your delivery is straight, the baulk-line will be obscured from above.

Fig 74   Jim tests the straightness of his cueing along the line where the green baize cushion meets the wooden cushion rail.

Fig 75   Jim can spot straight away that his cue action is pushing out to the right.

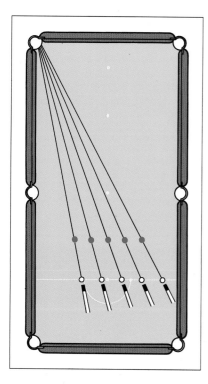

Fig 76   *The practice exercise used to promote straight cueing.*

Even if you are hitting the cue-ball in the centre, there is no guarantee that no unintentional side-spin will be imparted. Side can still be applied if the cue hits across the white, not striking through it in a straight line. After practising the baulk-line exercise, try some straight pots. Make each shot perfectly straight and try to pot the object-ball into the top pocket. Obviously, if the pot goes in, the shot has been played correctly. If you miss, however, just stay down over the shot.

STAR TIP

The main motivation for any sportsman is to attempt to raise his standard all the time. That's what keeps me interested in practice. It's impossible to be perfect but there's no harm in trying.
(Steve Davis, following his 1989 World Championship triumph)

Fig 77   *Practice – what it's all about. Steve Davis reaps the reward – here the 1988 World Championship Trophy.*

Do not move the cue until you have found out whether it is pointing at the middle of the aimed-for pocket. If, as is likely, it is not, then you know you are not cueing straight.

When you reach a point where you begin to feel you are cueing accurately, start to set targets for yourself. Move the object-ball nearer to the pocket and you will learn rapidly that as the distance between cue-ball and object-ball increases, so does the toughness of the pot.

STAR TIP

If you run your hand along the cloth towards the top of the cushion, you will notice that it feels far smoother than if you do so towards the baulk.
(Rex Williams, *How to become a Champion*)

This is a good solid practice routine which is certain to improve your cueing, and therefore your potting, if used on a regular basis.

Steve Davis, whose quest for technical

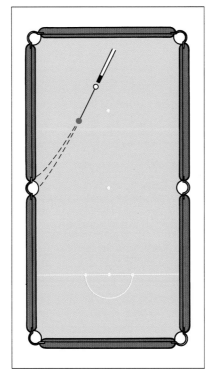

Fig 78   The effect of the nap on the path of the object-ball going towards the bottom cushion. (The effect is exaggerated due to the scale of the diagram.)

perfection is well known, has used this exercise daily all through his playing career as he maintains, quite rightly, that without straight cueing a consistently high standard of potting is impossible to accomplish.

The Effects of the Nap on Potting

The nap of the cloth has often been likened to the grain in a piece of wood. As the nap runs from the baulk end of the table towards the top cushion, the path of most shots is influenced by it in some degree.

In the majority of cases this effect is not pronounced, but it does come into play when shots of slow pace are being attempted into the centre pockets. If you are trying to roll the object-ball into a centre pocket from the top end of the table, the ball should be aimed at the far-jaw, as the nap tends to pull it towards the near jaw.

The amount of 'pull' will be directly linked to the heaviness of the cloth. If a table is worn, the effect of the nap will be small, whereas the pull of a newer cloth will be more severe.

CHAPTER 8

USING THE REST

At times, the position of the balls makes it impossible to reach a certain shot without some outside artificial aid, which in snooker is called the rest. Technique and confidence play an equal part when attempting a shot with the rest, and because of their lack of the latter many good players – including three times World Champion, John Spencer – count rest play as a major weakness in their overall game.

The Rest

There is a tendency for novices to use the rest 'tall way up', but this is wrong except, possibly, for the rare occasions where you need to strike the cue-ball very high. The shallow 'V' is preferable, for it allows the cue-ball to be hit dead-centre by a cue running almost horizontally to the bed of the table.

Fig 79   Front view, showing optimum distance between rest-head and cue-ball.

The first thing to do when using the rest is to make doubly sure that the equipment itself is giving you the best possible chance. The best rests have a tight 'V' for the cue to slide in, while the worst have a wobbly U. If there is more than one rest available in the room, select the best.

The orthodox grip used in normal circumstances is abandoned when using the rest. Instead, two fingers should be placed on the top end of the cue-butt with the thumb lending support underneath.

The hand which normally makes the bridge should be used to anchor the rest to the table so that its movement is kept to a minimum.

Whereas a shot with a normal bridge is made with the right elbow positioned behind the cue, a shot with the rest is made with the elbow swinging sideways to the cue. With this sideways swing it is more difficult to cue straight, but, with practice, it can be managed to the extent that you will be able to play almost as well with the rest as when using a normal bridge.

You should still be sideways to the shot, but the stance is reminiscent of the tennis backhand rather than the forehand. It is not easy to deliver the cue straight through in this position, but most people

Fig 80   The rest is used with the shallow 'V' for most shots.

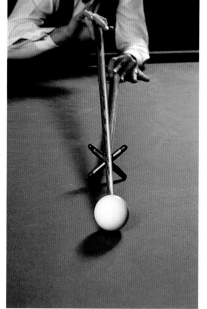

Fig 81   Despite Jim's side-on rest stance, his alignment is much the same as for a normal shot. Some players put the rest stem under the cue as an extra alignment guide.

Fig 82   Notice Jim's pen-like grip of the cue when using the
rest. The hand normally used to make a bridge anchors the
rest to the surface of the table.

Fig 83   Feet are spread further apart.
Stance is akin to that of a tennis
backhand.

Fig 84   Because the stance is sideways on, it is inevitable that
the right elbow (for a right-hander) juts out. The hinge closes
in front of the chest, not by the player's side – as happens on
normal shots.

find it easier if they remember to keep the
right elbow up, so that the lower arm is
horizontal to the bed of the table.

When using the rest you must try to
build up a smooth rhythm by taking a few
preliminary addresses at the cue-ball
before going ahead with the shot. Above
all, keep still as you make the actual stroke.

It is not advisable to try complicated
positional shots, particularly those
involving the use of cue-power, with the
rest. Remember that when you attempt a
screw shot using your normal bridge, the
bridge has to be lowered. This is not
possible with a rest-head, so deep screw
shots can only be played by hitting down
into the cue-ball, a situation which
inevitably leads to many miscues.

Half and Three-Quarter Butts

These are specially extended rests which
allow a player to reach almost the whole
length of the table. They also come with
an equally long cue, as a normal-length cue
would not be able to reach. In recent

Fig 85   Mark Bennett adopts the sideways grip and cueing action to play with the rest.

Fig 86   Even the professionals only attempt the simplest of shots when they are forced into using the spider.

times, however, these cumbersome and often badly maintained long cues have been made redundant by a relatively new addition to the list of snooker equipment, the cue extension.

These are extremely useful in that they allow a shot with the long rests to be played using your own familiar cue-tip.

The Spider

The spider, the most dreaded of the rests, is brought into action when the cue-ball is so placed that it cannot be reached using your normal stance and bridge, or when an intervening ball (or balls) prevents you from using the standard rest.

As when using the rest, anchor the spider securely to the table with your left hand. Never attempt anything ambitious when using this implement as even the most simple shot can easily go disastrously wrong.

CHAPTER 9

CORRECTING FAULTS, PRACTICE EXERCISES AND SKILL-DEVELOPING IDEAS

The limit of a player's development usually depends on the quality of his basic technique – straight cueing, stillness on the shot, accurate striking of the cue-ball and other dull-sounding but vital attributes. If, for example, after a great deal of practice you find fundamental shots such as stun and screw difficult to master, or if certain types of pots seem beyond you, it is time to return to the basics. Are you standing correctly? Is your bridge firm? Is your cueing accurate?

Practice Exercises

The best way to discover the answer to that last question is to place the cue-ball on the brown spot and try to hit it up and down the table off the top cushion over the line of the black, pink and blue spots. If the cue-ball strays to the right or left after making contact with the top cushion, you will know that some unintentional side-spin has been applied. A number of factors, including a poor stance, movement on the shot or bad alignment,

Fig 87   Test the straightness of your cueing by attempting to pot the blue off its spot into one of the four corner pockets, with the white anything over 2ft (61cm) away.

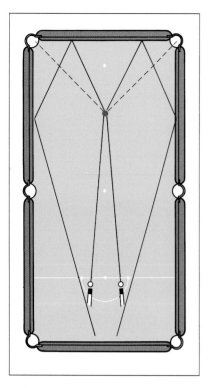

Fig 88   Good practice for 'angled' pots.

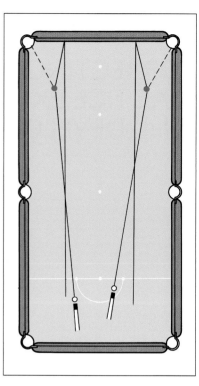

Fig 89   Almost-straight shots should be struck fuller than you think.

straight. Again, play a series of these. If you are missing consistently, the chances are that you are allowing too much angle (overcutting) and are making the object-ball strike several inches up the side cushion.

These 'almost straight shots' tend to be even straighter than you first think and it can take much self-discipline to adjust to the fact that the initial eyesight assessment of this angle has been incorrect. Concentrate on hitting this shot fuller and fuller, until, with practice, the correct angle is imprinted so deeply on your mind that the correct assessment of the angle becomes subconscious. It always pays in snooker to work on your weaknesses without neglecting to develop your strengths.

could lead to problems of this nature arising. Fred Davis, a man who placed a premium on accurate striking, favoured this exercise to the point where it filled up a large proportion of his practice time before major events. If, as he did, you work out how to eradicate the side yourself, that is fine. If not, the advice of a better player or even a professional coach will in most cases be very useful.

We saw in the previous chapter that straight cueing could be developed by potting a lengthy series of dead-straight pots but what about the myriad of angled pots that you will face?

To practise angled pots, put a ball on the pink spot and the cue-ball just inside either the yellow or green spots. It is essential to practise these shots from both sides of the table; otherwise, you may develop a preference for one side or the other as some slight irregularity in your stance or sighting creeps in.

Many players have particular difficulty with shots which are almost, but not quite,

Fig 90   Place the reds in a straight line across the table and play a series of straight (full-ball) pots into the facing corner pocket.

Fig 91 The 'line-up', snooker's most popular practice exercise. It hones touch, aids positional play and, by doing so, improves a player's break-building capabilities. It is also an ideal exercise for 10 or 15 minutes before a match to get any remaining cobwebs out of the system.

The Line-Up

The most popular solo practice routine, the line-up, helps potting and develops fluency. Place the colours on their spots before spacing the reds in a straight line between them. The most common variation of the line-up sees the reds about 2in (5cm) apart, spaced between the top cushion and the blue spot. However, the way you space them depends entirely on your own individual needs. The idea is to compile a break as normal – i.e. red, black, red – but this time, only the ball potted must be disturbed. This rule is designed to discipline yourself into accurate cue-ball control.

Professional Advice

Doug Mountjoy is the classic example of a man whose ailing career was revitalized with the help of a coach, Frank Callan – also an adviser to many leading players such as Steve Davis, Terry Griffiths and John Parrott – who recognized the causes of Mountjoy's slump to twenty-fourth on the World Ranking list. In December 1988, less than ten months after the pair had first met, Mountjoy astonished the world of snooker by capturing the Tennents UK Open title, worth £80,000.

Afterwards, Mountjoy said: 'It's difficult on your own to find out what you're doing wrong. I went to Frank Callan. He's helped me so much. Without that guy I'm nothing.'

LINE-UP PRACTICE

The great beauty of the line-up is that by keeping a mental note of your scores you have tangible evidence of your improvement, or lack of it. As an up-and-coming amateur at the Lucania Snooker Club, Romford, Steve Davis employed the line-up as a significant part of his practice sessions. In order to spur himself on, Davis would refuse food or drink until he had made a total clearance. The reward for a century was a chocolate bar or a cup of tea. Only a handful of ultra-dedicated enthusiasts would ever dream of going to such extremes, but the point of the story is that determined, single-minded practice reaps great benefits.

COACHING

A coach may have a strong influence on a player's psyche if the player concerned believes in the coach's judgement and is willing to learn.

Gary Hill, a twenty-year old amateur from Tipton in the West Midlands, began to experience problems with his preliminary addresses of the cue-ball. Quite often, he would unintentionally 'feather' the white with his cue-tip, causing expensive foul shots.

Wisely, he sought the guidance of Ken Garlick, an accomplished coach, at the Dudley Snooker Centre. Garlick stopped the feathering problem by suggesting that Hill should take his bridge-hand slightly further away from the cue-ball.

Six months later, at the World Junior Championship in Iceland, Hill found himself needing just the final black to make a maximum 147 break in one of his round robin matches.

'When I got over the black, all I could think about was not feathering the white. I remembered what Ken had told me and pulled my bridge-hand back slightly from the cue-ball', he said.

The black was duly potted and Hill became only the second amateur to compile a maximum in competition.

STAR TIP

My coach, Jim Meadowcroft, would explain something I was doing naturally, like the pause in the final backswing, so that I actually understood what I was doing. I had all the basics pretty well from the start. I played plain-ball at first, then someone in the club taught me how to screw a ball and I went from there.

(Allison Fisher, talking in *Snooker Scene* 1986)

PART 3
TACTICS

CHAPTER 10

BREAKBUILDING

The size of an amateur's highest break is very often the criterium by which he is rated. Someone who has made a 50 break is considered reasonable while a 100 break merchant is looked upon as something special. Breakbuilding skills do not guarantee success in themselves, but a player cannot reach the top level without them.

The century break, once a rarity, now crops up fairly frequently in the better classes of local league snooker, whilst amateur competitors and professionals make so many that they no longer bother to count them.

Breakbuilding is a game within a game with a player often gaining as much, or even more pleasure from beating his own

Fig 92   Breakbuilding – John Spencer, one of the game's great breakbuilders in the seventies.

Fig 93   Ray Reardon took to wearing glasses in his fifties.

personal best break as he would from winning a particular frame.

This chapter aims to outline the best approach to breakbuilding.

Red/Black Breakbuilding

Top players do succeed in potting balls from improbable angles, but all rely primarily on compiling a break with a series of easy shots once they are in. Whenever a competent player is left in a position similar to the one shown in Fig 94, where the black is on its spot and there are three pottable reds in close proximity, he thinks: 'I've got at least twenty-four points here for the taking unless I do something stupid.'

Good players rarely play any shot without a clear idea of what their next move is going to be. Generally, the less experienced the player, the less precisely he will be able to control the cue-ball.

Nevertheless, certain obvious principles, such as keeping the cue-ball off the cushion and avoiding having to bridge over a ball, should be observed.

Around the black spot, two other factors are particularly important:

1. Clear the paths between the black spot and the two top pockets.
2. Avoid leaving the cue-ball straight on the black.

If you study the shots needed to complete the three-reds/three-blacks sequence in Fig 94, you will notice that the break revolves around two basic ploys:

1. Leaving an angle on the black.
2. Stunning out to leave the cue-ball nicely positioned for the next red.

The diagram shows the sequence being completed without the cue-ball touching the cushion, but there is such a large margin of error that you can use the

cushions to help you keep in position, if necessary.

There is nothing intrinsically wrong in using the cushions for position, but it is important to master the technique of leaving an angle on the black and stunning up the table, because you will need this skill in controlling the cue-ball in a confined area. The balls will not always be nicely spaced out (as here). More often, there will be pottable reds mingled with unpottable and awkward reds.

Fig 95 demonstrates an important element in building a break – choice of shot – which depends less on technical factors than on experience and common sense. On the face of it, there is a choice between red A and red B, either of which is easy to pot in such a way as to leave a perfect position on the black. However, looking further ahead, it becomes obvious that red B is the better bet, because it leaves the black more open for later stages in the break.

Fig 96 also presents a choice between

Fig 94

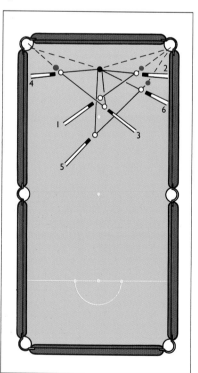

Fig 95

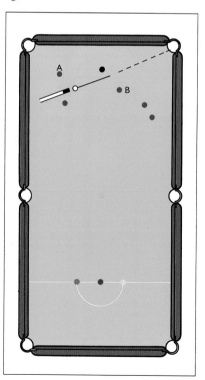

Fig 96

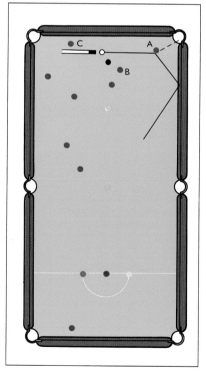

ball off the top and side cushions and leave the pink in the middle, but you would still have the problem of red A blocking the black's path to one top pocket later in the break. In short, it stands to reason that it is much easier to build a break round the black spot if the black is pottable into both pockets.

Breakbuilding with Other Colours

Although the black plays an important part in most big breaks, there are many occasions when it is tied up among a cluster of other balls or is awkwardly placed on a cushion. There are, in addition, countless occasions when the position of the other balls makes it impossible, or not worthwhile, to attempt to get position on the black.

The blue is often an invaluable ball with which to link a break together. As Fig 98 shows, the black and pink are hemmed in

Fig 98

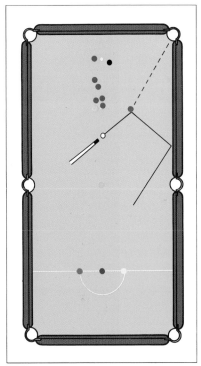

Fig 97   Here, the reds indicate the line that the blue will take into the middle pocket after Jim has doubled it off the side cushion.

reds. Red B is in the same position as in Fig 95 and is a high priority in order to give room for manoeuvre round the black. However, because B is not pottable yet, you will have to wait your chance for this

ball and, meanwhile, from the available choice of red, take red A with a little screw and right-hand side to leave position on the pink. By potting red C, it would have been possible to run the cue-

Fig 99   Steve Davis has struck the cue-ball and sent the blue towards the pocket.
The cue-ball has moved to his right and the blue to his left, but note how he has
maintained stillness of the shot and how his cue has not deviated from its original line.

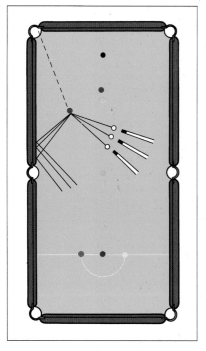

Fig 100

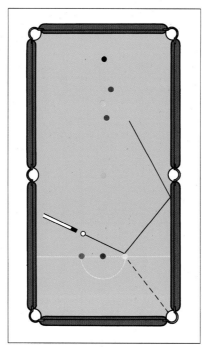

Fig 101

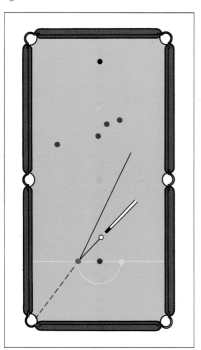

Fig 102

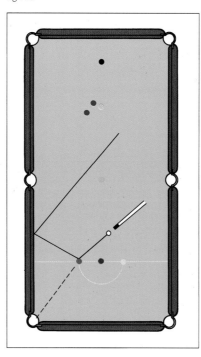

Fig 103

and thus, in potting the red, the idea is to get position slightly baulk-side of the blue, so that you can easily take the cue-ball up for another loose red. Play with screw and a little right-hand side to widen the angle that the cue-ball takes when it hits the side cushion. If you play without this touch of side, you will have to screw nearer the middle pocket (which can be a dangerous thing to do if you slightly overscrew) or bring the cue-ball further away from the side cushion, in towards the blue (which can leave you too close to the blue and force you to pot it at an acute angle).

There are countless variations on this type of shot, which are well worth some systematic practice. Practise potting reds (*see* Fig 100) into the corner pocket from all angles between quarter- to three-quarter ball to leave an identical position on the blue. The thinner screws require very good touch, as you will need to make the screw and side bite sharply, even though you will be hitting the cue-ball quite softly.

It is also useful to practise screwing up the table for the reds from the baulk colours: the yellow, green and brown (*see* Fig 101). Because the cue-ball is travelling several feet, its final position is more difficult to gauge than for a shorter distance, but again, with practice, a fair degree of control can be obtained. Screwing off the green and yellow is frequently preferable to screwing off the brown, as the middle pocket all too often seems to get in the way.

Fig 102 shows a straightforward screw back from a three-quarter ball contact on the green. In Fig 103, however, the different angle on the green (i.e. half-ball instead of three-quarter ball) means that you will have to use the side cushion. Play this shot with screw and some right-hand side, but be careful not to overdo the latter, as the remaining red will not be pottable if the cue-ball runs much further than the position shown in the diagram. Fig 104 is another three-quarter ball pot on the green, but this time the position of the two remaining reds – between the pink and black spots – makes it necessary to play the run through instead of the screw back. Make sure you strike the cue-ball

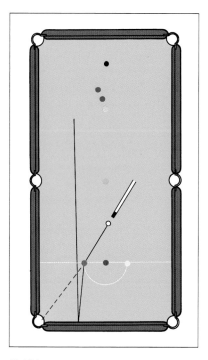

Fig 104

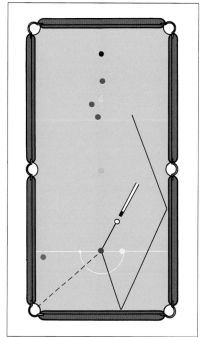

Fig 105

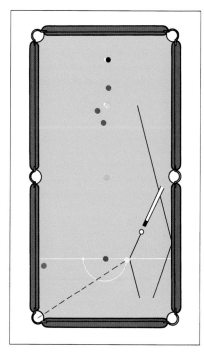

Fig 106

well above centre. Unintentional stun or inadvertent use of a little left-hand side (check) will restrict the run of the cue-ball and leave it short of the desired position on the reds.

Fig 105 shows the brown being potted with a touch of left-hand side to swing the cue-ball off the baulk and side cushions in towards the remaining two reds. Without the side, the cue-ball would finish much nearer the side cushion and make your next shot more difficult. Most good players in fact prefer, if there is a choice, to play positional shots which bring the cue-ball away from a cushion towards the next object-ball, rather than shots in which the cue-ball is travelling towards a cushion.

Fig 106 is similar to Fig 105 – your choice of the yellow is determined by the fact that a straight screw back from the brown will land the cue-ball in the middle pocket.

During breaks, you will often need to split up a bunch of reds which have remained in a loosely triangular shape behind the pink spot. A powerful stun shot while potting the black from its spot is the

Fig 107   Standard pack disturbance – stun shot off the black.

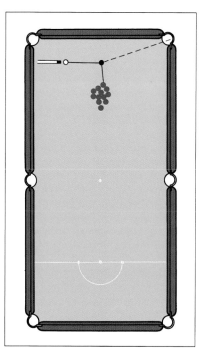

Fig 108   Making contact with the pink to split the reds.

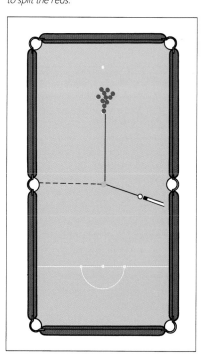

simplest way to do this, but if the black is unavailable other alternatives must be found.

Stunning the white towards the pack after potting the blue into a centre pocket is a possible way of disturbing the reds to send them into pottable positions, but it is a shot which requires pin-point accuracy.

The reds usually break best if the white is sent into the pink (on its spot) or into the top red of the pyramid. If the cue-ball makes contact with the 'back reds' it has the tendency to slide off towards a corner pocket. The reds tend to move less if this happens and the possibility of an in-off into a top pocket is greatly increased.

Screw and running side when potting the yellow or green from the positions shown in Fig 110 also has the desired effect of taking the cue-ball into the reds. However, this shot is made difficult by the large amount of cue power required.

Doubles, Sets and Plants

Doubles

Fig 111 shows five positions in which it is possible either to start or to continue a break by means of a double. This entails playing the object-ball into a cushion at such an angle that it will rebound into a pocket. Shot 1 is one of the easiest doubles on the table, since the object-ball is near enough the middle pocket to provide a reference point for the opposite middle pocket, into which you hope the object ball will rebound.

Most professionals and good amateurs would be successful with shot 1 nine times out of ten, for the half-ball angle is easy to assess. So too is the full-ball contact in shot 2, where the pack of the cue-ball to the object-ball and of the object-ball from the cushion to the middle pocket makes a perfect 'V'.

Double angles are much more difficult to assess if the object-ball is further away from the middle pocket and even more so if the angle at which the cue-ball must strike the object-ball is not immediately

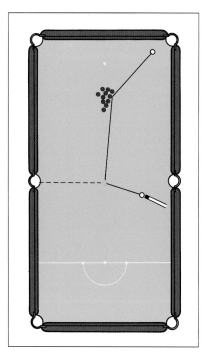

Fig 109   Making contact with the 'back reds' causes the cue-ball to slide off.

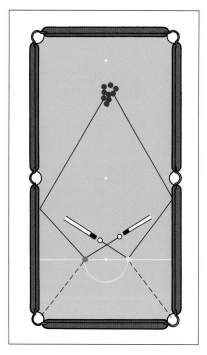

Fig 110   Splitting pack off yellow or green.

Fig 111

obvious. For instance, in shot 5, the object-ball is a little way off the side cushion, so the drill is to work out the cue-ball/object-ball contact, which will put the object-ball on the 'V'-shaped line necessary to complete the double. This looks easy enough on the diagram, but in practice, selecting the exact spot which the object-ball should strike on a long length of cushion is very difficult.

This leads on to good general rule to adopt in almost any double you play, namely: do not attempt a double unless it is likely that the cue-ball will run into a safe position.

Shot 3 in this diagram, a species known as a cut back double, often offers a chance of safety coupled with a pot, since the cue-ball, in going across the object-ball to make the correct doubling contact, will then run down towards the baulk cushion.

Doubles in which the object-ball enters a corner pocket after striking a side cushion are more difficult to gauge than middle pocket doubles and in most cases such doubles represent a greater risk,

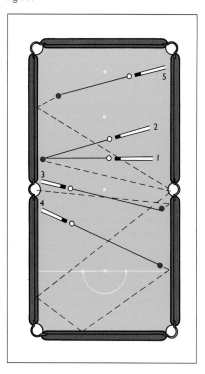

since the cue-ball tends to remain somewhere in the middle of the table. If this is so, there cannot be more than 6 or 7ft (1.8 or 2.1m) between the cue-ball and the object-ball for your opponent's next shot, a distance (or lack of it) which puts the odds in your opponent's favour.

Often, a preferable alternative to the corner pocket double is the cocked hat double, shown in shot 4. Here, the object-ball is sent off the baulk and side cushions to enter the middle pocket, while the cue-ball – struck above centre – will run through so that it finishes somewhere near the baulk cushion. This is not as difficult as it looks, because the assessment of the angle depends on your being able to visualize the object-ball completing three sides of a rectangle (as shown) with part of the side cushion acting as the fourth side.

Some of the shots in Fig 111 strongly imply that doubles can be played as 'shots to nothing', but Figs 113 and 114 make this more explicit. In Fig 113, the safety shot from the pack of reds down the table towards the baulk cushion is not going to put your opponent in trouble and, indeed, it may well give him an opening, because some reds are in the bottom half of the table. Therefore, the shot you should play here is to double the red as shown. If successful, you will have a good position on the black; if unsuccessful, there will be nothing left for your opponent, even though you would not actually put him in trouble.

In Fig 114 it is possible to combine an attempt at a double with a really aggressive safety stroke. This crossed double, so-called because the cue-ball goes across the object-ball, doubles a red towards (and hopefully into) the corner pocket, while the cue-ball bounces off the top cushion to return somewhere near the baulk cushion. If the red goes in, the green will be available to continue the break; if it does not, your opponent will have to play a tricky safety shot.

Sets and Plants

Sets and plants can occur at any time in a frame but they most frequently occur when there is a cluster of reds between the pink and black spots. A set occurs

Fig 112   Jim sizes up a simple plant. The cue-ball will strike the red nearest to it, which, in turn, will hit the second red in such a way that it is potted.

Fig 113

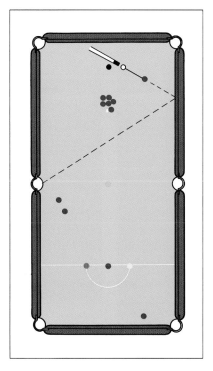

Fig 114

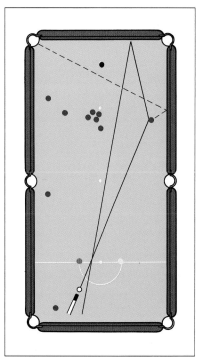

Fig 115   Jim plays a set. The difference between this and a plant is that the two reds are touching.

Fig 116   Looking at it, it would seem logical to hit this set on the right-hand side. However, because of the transference of side-spin, the white (as shown by Jim) must strike the red on its left to squeeze the second red into the pocket.

Fig 117   Cliff Thorburn strikes downwards on the cue-ball near a cushion to obtain backspin.

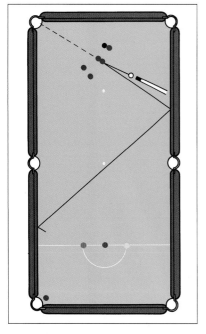

Fig 118

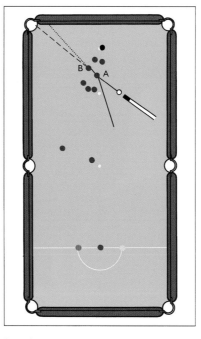

Fig 119

Fig 120

when two object-balls are touching in such a way that, when contacted by the cue-ball at almost any angle, the second object-ball will be potted. One must emphasize 'almost any angle', because a very thin contact creates something akin to a squeeze effect, which leads the second object-ball to miss the pocket by a couple of inches. Usually, the most difficult element in this shot is overcome merely by recognizing that a set is there – something which is not always obvious when there are many balls clustered nearby.

As with an ordinary pot, you should not be content simply with potting the second object-ball; play for position to continue the break. If you are playing a screw back as in Fig 118, bear in mind that the cue-ball is in effect striking an object-ball which is twice as heavy, since the two reds offer twice as much resistance to the initial impact of the object-ball than is ordinarily the case with one red. This means that it is possible to screw back much further with less effort.

Fig 119 shows an example of a plant, a type of shot generally more difficult than a set because the two object-balls are not

touching and thus have to strike each other at a particular angle for the pot to be completed. The best way of assessing

these angles is to imagine for a moment that the first object-ball is, in fact, the cue-ball. For example, shape up to red A in Fig 120 as if it were the cue-ball, and thus set the fact that you will need a three-quarter ball contact on red B to pot it.

Continue an imaginary line through the point of contact towards the cushion and try to memorize the point at which red A would strike the cushion if red B were not in the way. You will need to bring your utmost concentration to bear on this when you return to the cue-ball and aim at red A. As with a set, play position from your attempted plant, in this case screwing back to take the blue into the middle pocket.

Years of practice and experience are necessary to become really proficient at plants, but even good players do not have a very high success rate with (and therefore do not often attempt) plants which involve anything below a half-ball contact. This is because the difficulty of gauging this type of shot is compounded by both object-balls, and the pocket cannot be kept more or less squarely in your main line of vision.

CHAPTER 11

CHOICE OF SHOT

What was said in the previous chapter on red/black break-building is also broadly true of the pink, blue and other balls. When you begin to think: 'Yes, if I take this red now, that other red will be pottable later in the break,' there is some justification for believing that you have the beginnings of a 'snooker brain'. In Fig 120, in the previous chapter, the choice of red is determined not by the need to create space around the black spot, but by the chance of allowing a greater margin for error in positional play. Red A is the ball to take here (not red C) because in doing so it becomes possible to pot red B into both top pockets instead of just one.

Fig 121

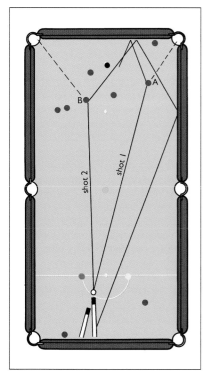

In any class of play, confidence in easy and not very difficult shots — both in potting and positional play — is more important long term than flashes of brilliance. More important still, if a player gradually builds up his confidence with easy shots, he is more likely to pot something difficult than if he has been missing shots he ought to get.

There are times when a player is forced into playing 'neck or nothing' shots, but generally speaking, it is wise to balance the risk of leaving an easy opening for your opponent against the possible gain if you

Fig 122   Choice of shot – Eddie Charlton ponders over what to do next.

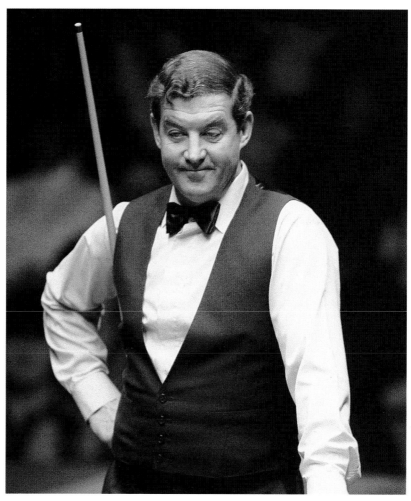

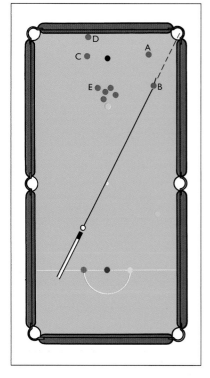

Fig 123

Fig 124

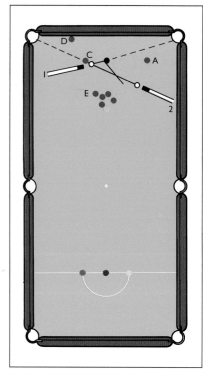

Fig 125

are successful with your initial shot. For instance, in Fig 121 some inexperienced players might attempt red A, rolling the cue-ball the length of the table, in order to pot the red slowly and stay on the black. Even if you sight the angle correctly and stroke the cue-ball perfectly (two big 'ifs'), the slightest imperfection in the table will cause the cue-ball to run off course before it reaches the red and thus ruin the shot. If this happens, your opponent has the choice of two easy shots and the chance of a useful break.

More Choice of Shots

There is, in fact, a choice of reds in Fig 123. Superficially, red A may seem preferable – it is nearer the pocket than red B and the cue-ball has only to bounce off the top cushion gently to finish in position for the black. The trouble is though, that gently played rolls, particularly when the cue-ball

has some distance to travel before contacting the object-ball, are exceedingly treacherous, not only – as we have seen – for potting, but also in controlling the cue-ball. Red B, however, is our old friend the straight pot. Stun this in – as you should if you are cueing straight – and you should go into the lead with a useful break. The angle on the black is such that you could pot it at speed, so that the cue-ball would rebound off the top cushion and scatter the reds, possibly paving the way for a really big break.

However, even top professionals would rarely split the pack so early in a break.

They would instead make sure of clearing the 'open' reds and, only when there was one or possibly two of these left, would they consider opening up the pack.

The theory behind this is that it is better to make as sure as one can of twenty or thirty points, rather than make eight and perhaps leave oneself in an impossible position. The angle on the black is such that reds C, D or A can easily be taken after it. D is the most difficult of the three, so it is sensible on most occasions to take the easier reds first. A is easy to play for, but C is the best choice (*see* Fig 124) by means of stunning the cue-ball on and off the top cushion, because potting C will leave the area around the black spot completely clear. This is likely to be important when you come to take red D.

Pot C with stun to leave a slight angle on the black, so that another stun will leave you in a position to take red A next (*see* Fig 126, shot 1). When you pot the black (Fig 125, shot 2), try to leave a position such that in potting A (*see* Fig 126, shot 1),

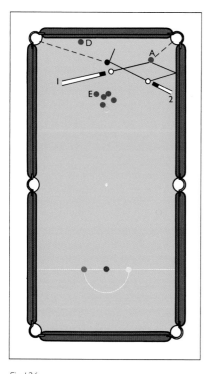

Fig 126

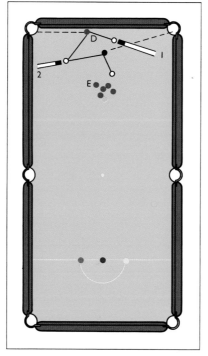

Fig 127

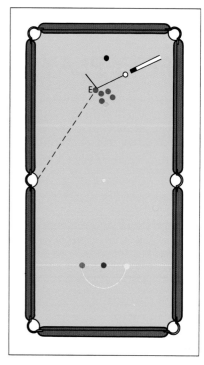

Fig 128

you will position the cue-ball at a slight angle on the black, so that you can take D along the cushion. This simple little shot shows that the secret behind the success of top players is often due to the position with which they control the cue-ball in easy shots, rather than their more spectacular feats with difficult shots.

In potting the black (*see* Fig 126, shot 2), play to leave a three-quarter ball red along the cushion. If you leave yourself straight on this red, it is impossible to obtain a good position on the black, and cuts along the cushion are notoriously difficult to gauge.

Pot red D firmly to leave position on the black (*see* Fig 127, shot 1), but do not be too eager to leave an angle to split the pack from the black. First, examine carefully whether there is a red which at first glance seems part of the pack, but which is in reality pottable. Red E is a typical example of this; it is almost part of the pack but is actually pottable in the middle pocket; thus, when potting the black, you should manoeuvre the cue-ball into a three-quarter angle to take red D (*see* Fig 127, shot 2).

These middle pocket pots are invaluable in keeping a break going, but they do need practice.

A controlled medium-paced shot with screw (*see* Fig 128), should leave you on the black with a good chance of splitting the reds. Splitting a large pack of reds is always to some extent a gamble, even if the cue-ball goes into them at a fair speed: the reds may split perfectly for a big break, or the cue-ball may end up in the middle of them with no way of scoring. There is good reason when this happens

to be thankful that you are already thirty or forty points ahead.

The correct choice of shots is essential for snooker success. Therefore, if you are unsure as to which shot to play in a certain position, do not hurriedly decide to play the first shot that comes to mind. Instead, work out all the available alternatives. Taking your time to think things through is a sensible ploy, but do not take on unnecessarily lengthy time, for that leads to indecisiveness and loss of rhythm. Once your mind is made up, concentrate fully on the shot in hand. Do not worry about whether your decision was the right one, it is too late for that.

CHAPTER 12

SAFETY PLAY

Apart from potting balls, the other vital ingredient in snooker is safety play, i.e. shots which make it difficult for your opponent to score points himself and which place him in awkward positions.

It is all very well to have excellent potting and breakbuilding skills, but if your safety play is poor, the chances of displaying these skills will be severely limited because your opponent will be getting most of the scoring opportunities.

Breaking Off

The first shot of a frame is very important. If you win the toss, always break off,

Fig 129

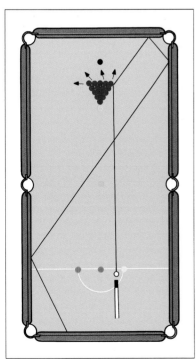

because it gives you a first class chance of taking the initiative straight away. The most reliable opening shot is to strike the outside red with right-hand side, to bring the cue-ball off three cushions to within 1in (2.5cm) or so of the baulk cushion behind the green (*see* Fig 129). Unless you are very careless (if, for example, you do not use enough right-hand side and the cue-ball collides with the blue) this shot cannot go seriously wrong and may well get your opponent off on the wrong foot by giving him a tricky first shot.

The Opening Exchanges

The opening exchanges in most frames consist of both players trying to get the cue-ball to return as near as possible to the baulk cushion, until one player either makes a mistake and leaves an opening, or takes a risk and tries to pot a red from a long distance. Occasionally, the reds may split from the opening shot in such a way that your opponent cannot make his return to the baulk cushion. In Fig 130 he does not have this problem, but he is seriously impeded by having the cue-ball right under the baulk cushion. It is difficult enough in any circumstance to play from under the cushion, since you can only hit the top part of the cue-ball, but the

difficulty is magnified when the object-ball is some distance away.

The answering shot in this tricky position is the very thin contact shot shown in Fig 130. At first glance, there seems to be grave danger of an in-off, but your billiards experience should tell you that the angle for this is almost half-ball. If you hit the shot much thinner, there is no danger of an in-off and the cue-ball, with good judgement of strength, should return near the baulk line.

This very thin escape occurs a great deal and is therefore one to be mastered. Indeed, most safety shots from the reds at this stage of the game are thinner than half-ball. Except when you are in extreme

Fig 130

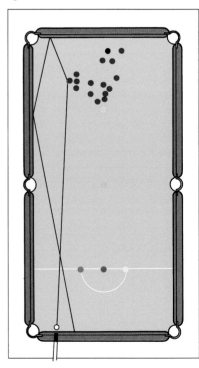

difficulty, always try to answer a good safety shot with a better one. There will be times when you must simply concentrate on preventing your opponent from scoring, but otherwise you should always play your safety shots constructively.

In Fig 131, for example, many players would play the thin return, (shot 1), which is correct as far as it goes, but which gives your opponent a chance to make a similar reply. Shot 2 is much better because, by playing with right-hand side, the cue-ball can be swung round off three cushions to the opposite side of the table, where the distribution of the reds is such that a return to the baulk cushion is impossible.

What can happen when a thicker than half-ball contact is made is shown in Fig 132, where the cue-ball has only returned half-way down the table and the more thickly-contacted red has disturbed the pack, leaving the type of middle-distance pot which often leads to a break.

Constructive Safety

There will be countless occasions when you find yourself near the pack of reds without a really good potting opening, but with an easy chance to leave the cue-ball on the baulk cushion for your opponent. Play these shots with care. Do not just send the cue-ball vaguely down the table, thinking it sufficient to prevent your opponent scoring – make things as difficult for him as you can! Get the cue-ball as near as possible to the baulk cushion; if you can get it behind one of the baulk colours, so much the better.

There are six shots in Fig 133, all of which should be played with the idea of putting the cue-ball as near to the baulk cushion as possible.

Shot 1 is a simple quarter- to half-ball flick off the end red, taking the cue-ball between the yellow and brown. In Shot 2, the angle is such that the direct route to the baulk cushion is impossible, so the shot must be played from the side cushion to

leave the cue-ball on the baulk cushion behind the yellow. Play this with a little screw and right-hand side.

Shot 3, in which the cue-ball is almost directly behind the pack, requires the use of right-hand side to widen the angle at which the cue-ball will leave the side cushion. This is necessary to avoid making contact with the yellow.

Shots 4, 5 and 6 duplicate shots 1, 2 and 3 from the other side of the table. None of them is difficult to execute, but there are clear advantages to be gained by those who play them with good touch: it is a great deal more difficult to play an answering safety shot if the cue-ball is tight on the baulk cushion than if it is 5 or 6ft (1.5 or 1.8m) away.

To conclude the hints on this important phase of the game, Fig 135, shot 1, shows the cue-ball being played with left-hand side to bring it off the two side cushions and level it dead on the baulk cushion. Shot 2 shows left-hand side being used to widen the angle that the cue-ball takes

Fig 131

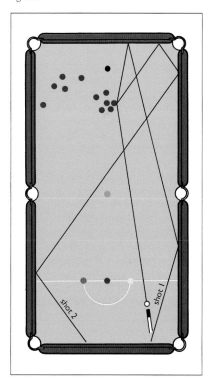

Fig 132

Fig 133

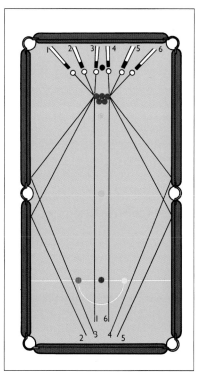

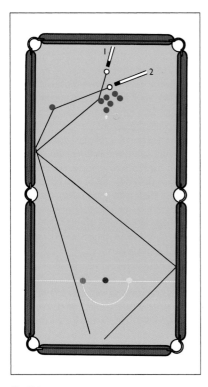

Fig 134

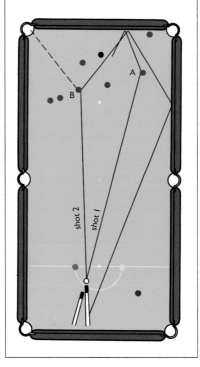

Fig 135

Fig 136

from the cushion to avoid a cannon on the green and to take it again to within one inch or so of the baulk cushion.

If you are as certain as you can be that you will not leave a pot available after playing a particular safety shot off the pack, always bear one thing in mind: if you try to split the reds up as much as possible, your break-building opportunities will be greater should your opponent make a mistake.

Shots to Nothing

In the sort of position shown in Fig 136, it is much more sensible to attempt red B. If you pot it, the brown, or (as the cue-ball has run slightly further) the pink, is available to continue your break; if you do not succeed, then at least the cue-ball will be near the baulk cushion, keeping your opponent at a distance from the reds.

These 'shots to nothing' – so-called because they offer the maximum gain for

the minimum risk – are often open to you very early in a frame, if you look for them. In Fig 136, for example, it may be not be immediately obvious that a red can be potted into the top pocket despite the cluster of reds around it. These shots to nothing call for good judgement of angles, since they will be completely spoiled if the cue-ball kisses other balls on route to the baulk cushion. Billiards players start with an advantage here, since they are so accustomed to attempting cannons that they are naturally more adept at avoiding them when they want to. In this particular case, you should attempt the pot with some right-hand side, both to help swing the cue-ball round the black and also to avoid kissing the blue on the way back down the table.

Snookering

Except at the end of a frame when the combined value of the balls remaining is

insufficient to win by potting alone, a snooker is usually a matter of tactics rather than a device for scoring points. Some players, particularly when they have lost their confidence, pay excessive attention to snookering, forgetting perhaps that in the end they have to pot balls to win.

However, there are also times when discretion is the better part of valour, as in Fig 137. Either through bad luck or bad judgement, you have potted a red and finished straight on both the green and yellow, so that, even with a deep screw, it is impossible to get the cue-ball up the table and in position for one of the remaining reds. You could either pot the yellow or the green and then attempt the red along the baulk cushion, but this is a dangerous shot. If played along the top cushion, the nap (which runs from baulk to black end) helps the object-ball hug the cushion. However, on the baulk cushion, the nap pulls the object-ball away from the cushion, so that the shot is more likely to be missed. Therefore, your shot is to pot

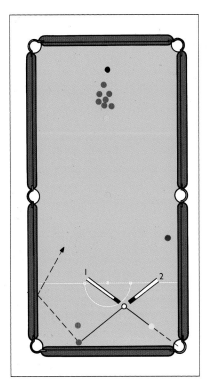

Fig 137

Fig 138

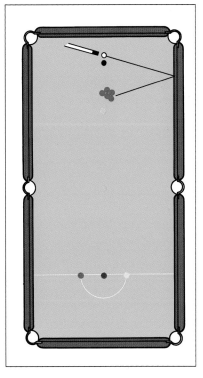

Fig 139

the yellow with a stun stroke and then to stun the red full to send it up the table, leaving the cue-ball behind the green.

This should prove a very nasty position for your opponent, because the worst snookers to negotiate are those where the object-balls are in the open with the obvious danger of conceding an opening for a break. Should your opponent also be on the cushion, this will intensify his difficulty – he will be unable to control the use of any side that he needs as accurately as if he had his bridge-hand on the table.

As explained earlier, shots to nothing on the reds are ideally those shots which will leave a colour on, if the red is potted, but which in any case leave your opponent dead-safe or snookered, if it is not. Sometimes, shots to nothing do not quite work out as planned and there may be no colour available to follow the red. Often, however, there is a very good alternative in rolling up slowly behind one of the baulk colours. Judgement of strength is the key to this shot. It is, of course, disastrous not

to reach the object-ball, for this will give your opponent the option either of taking a free ball, or of asking you to play again. On the other hand, the point of the shot is lost if it is played too hard.

Look carefully at the distribution of the reds before you play a roll up. It can often be, as in Fig 138, that the escape from one side cushion (here, the right), is into a tight pack of reds, while the escape from the other cushion is more dangerous, because some reds are open and pottable. Unless you can leave the cue-ball almost touching the brown, so that both escape routes are blocked, it is good policy in this type of position to play the cue-ball from the yellow in order to leave it behind the green.

This will make your opponent use the left-hand side cushion, where the open reds are, or play a more complex two-cushion escape using baulk and side cushions. He will need to be a good player to play the latter accurately enough to deny you an opening.

Snooker Escapes

The basic rule in escaping from snookers is to roll up slowly to balls which are not pottable and to make firm contact with balls which are, in order to have a chance of putting them safe.

In Fig 139, all you have to do is pick your spot on the side cushion and roll up to the reds. You cannot put your opponent in trouble like this, but at least he has to play another good shot to put you in trouble. Quite the worst thing to do is to scatter the reds and present him with a break. However, when the snookered red at which you are playing is in the open, it is clearly madness to roll up to it slowly, for even if you hit it, you will leave it on for your opponent. It is much better to play this escape briskly (*see* Fig 141). If you miss the red, the cue-ball will at least be travelling further away from it for your opponent. If you hit it, the force of the contact should again put some distance between the two balls.

Fig 140   John Parrott plays from tight on a baulk cushion.

As shown in Fig 142, you will frequently find it advantageous, when snookered, to attempt to escape onto a difficult isolated red (shot 2) rather than onto a more obvious red or group of reds (shot 1). You must attempt to escape from snookers, but it is often better to risk giving away four points and leaving your opponent safe, rather than to negotiate snooker and leave your opponent with a frame-winning break. In Fig 142, for example, it is clearly wise to try to hit the 'safe' red on the cushion rather than the open reds round the pink spot.

The Swerve Shot

This shot sometimes provides an alternative method of escape and it is best employed when the snooker is on to a single ball and other balls are blocking the orthodox use of cushions (see Fig 143). The technique of swerving the cue-ball involves raising the butt of the cue and striking a sharp glancing blow at the left-hand side of the cue-ball (or right-hand side, as the case may be). The ordinary effect of using side (i.e. the cue-ball pushing out to the right before spinning to the left) will be exaggerated both by the downward angle at which the cue meets the cue-ball and by the tip going across the cue-ball rather than through it. Aim just to miss the intervening ball and, as it passes it, the 'second phase' spin should start to operate and swerve the cue-ball to the right.

The final position of the balls is even more difficult to predict with a swerve shot than with other escapes, but, with any luck at all, the cue-ball and the object-ball should at least finish some distance apart.

One final point about snookering: watch the scoreboard! If you are, for example, thirty-two points behind on the yellow (i.e. with only twenty-seven 'potting' points left on the table) then you need two snookers to win. However, if you pot yellow, green and brown, this makes you twenty-three

behind with only eighteen points on the table. You thus need only one snooker to draw, because the minimum penalty on the table is now five. Much depends on the precise position of the balls, but in Fig 144 you should take yellow, green and brown, as shown, and then manoeuvre the cue-ball into position to leave a very nasty snooker behind the black. Your opponent may by now feel a little nervous and he can no longer afford to miss the blue. You have already taken three of the six balls you need to keep in the game.

Leading on from this, it is a common mistake, as soon as your opponent needs two snookers or even one, to start trickling balls over the pocket, the

Fig 141

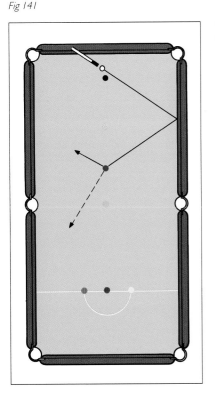

Fig 142

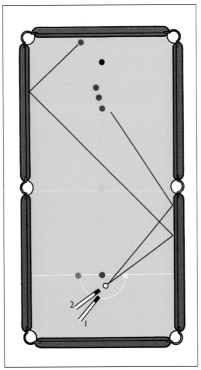

Fig 143

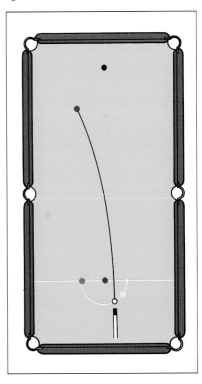

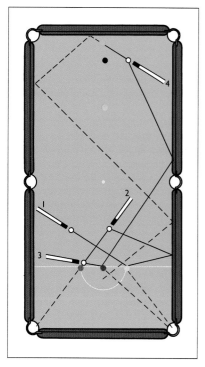

Fig 144

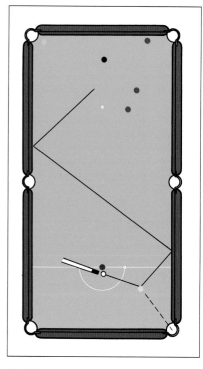

Fig 145

misguided theory being that if you make your opponent pot all the remaining balls, he cannot win. If only the pink and black remain, this argument is flawless, but, if a number of colours remain, what generally happens is that your opponent accepts the free gifts and then snookers you. Do not forget, if your opponent needs snookers, he not only has to get them (and you have to miss them) but he must also pot all the balls. Do not do half the job for him!

Another common mistake when a player fails to escape from a snooker and leaves another snooker position is for his opponent to ask him to play again. Sometimes, this is a sound enough decision but, as in Fig 145, it is a mistake to take this step too hastily. It is true that this snooker is a very nasty one, but even so, it would still be better to exercise your option to take a free ball.

Nominate yellow as your free ball and

screw up the table for the pink. There are several reds open in the top part of the table and you should, therefore, finish the game with a useful break.

If, on the other hand, you were to ask your opponent to play again, he could possibly leave you safe (even if he gives another four away) and you might not have the same good opening again. When there is a reasonable chance, always attack.

HINTS ON MATCHPLAY

Even if you have thoroughly absorbed the entire contents of this book, there will be many things that you will only find out through regular playing on all types of tables and against a wide variety of opponents. Meanwhile, here are a few hints on how to make the best of the skill you have acquired, in any competitive matches you may play.

First, assuming that you have long since fulfilled the minimum requirement of buying one cue and sticking to it, make sure that you maintain it in the best possible condition. Keep it in a cue case, of course, and be careful not to leave it somewhere exceptionally warm (e.g. leaning up against a radiator) or exceptionally cold (e.g. overnight in the middle of winter in the back of a car). In either case, the cue will probably warp. An occasional wipe-down with a slightly damp cloth is also recommended, as a sticky cue does not advance fluency in cueing.

Once you have made sure that the tip of your cue is neither rock-hard nor spongy, check that it is domed, so that its roundness grips the shape of the ball – something that is impossible with a flat tip. Constant chalking (most top players chalk their cue every two or three shots) can lead to a build-up of chalk on the tip, which needs to be broken off by pressing a file into it in order to leave a slightly

Fig 146 Cliff Thorburn, chalking his cue during a match.

KIT CHECK

You can be the owner of the most expensive cue currently available, but if its tip is shiny, mushroomed, spongy, or flat, it will be impossible to play at a high standard.

abrasive surface. If you do not do this, a shiny surface is gradually created and miscues tend to become more frequent.

Always carry your own block of chalk with you because a cue-tip does not take kindly to having several different varieties applied to it in quick succession. Use chalk which stays on the tip and does not fly off in great clouds when the tip strikes the cue-ball. In my experience, green National Tournament or Triangle Chalk, manufactured in the US, is the best type to use. Top players prefer the green chalk because it does not stick to the cue-ball. Chalk and other unwanted substances on the cue-ball and object-ball have been cited as the major reason for the dreaded

kick (a bad contact between the balls which causes them to fly off at unpredictable angles).

On the evening of a match, always leave yourself enough time to reach the appointed venue without having to make a last minute dash. There is nothing worse than having to start a match a minute or so after reaching a club, without giving yourself a chance to become composed.

Do not eat a big meal before you play. A heavy meal tends to dull the senses and, once your nerves start to play up in the middle of a match, you may start to feel uncomfortable. This in itself is a distraction you can ill afford.

Try to approach each match, at whatever level, with the idea that you are going to play your very best in relation to the positions which may come your way. A tournament golfer is, in a way, competing against other golfers, but, in essence, he is competing against the course, trying to get round in the least number of shots. This should be your philosophy in that you should concentrate less on what your opponent is doing than

on what you yourself are doing. This is of course easier said than done, but it will certainly be to your advantage, particularly when things are tense, to concentrate on seeing the shots as they really are without letting thoughts of their consequences intrude. As soon as you start to think 'I've only got to pot yellow and green and he can't win', you are dissipating your concentration on the shot in hand. These thoughts are inevitable, but the trick is to get rid of them before you actually settle down to play the shot.

Similarly, if you start to play a pot with two or three ideas in your mind about what you are attempting to do positionally, there is every chance that the pot will be missed. Clarity of thought

KIT CHECK

At times, running repairs during a match need to be carried out on a tip. Because of this, make sure that you always carry a file in your cue case.

Fig 147   Steve Davis – a study in concentration.

Fig 148   Bill Werbeniuk – an exception to the alcohol rule.

Fig 149 Neil Foulds studies a tricky position.

before you actually get down to play the shot is essential. If you find yourself down on a shot and are still uncertain about what you are trying to do, you should get up, maybe chalk your cue, and consider the matter until your intentions are clear.

Above all, enjoy the game. Enjoy the close matches as well as the easy ones, learn from your mistakes if you can and try to analyze how good players approach individual situations.

Fitness

While it is obvious that snooker and billiards do not require the same level of physical fitness as sports such as squash, tennis, athletics or football do, it would be unwise to dismiss the need for fitness altogether.

Some professional matches are contested over marathon distances of seventeen, nineteen or even thirty-five frames and they often develop into gruelling affairs involving many hours of continuous play. If you believe that 'a healthy body makes a healthy mind' the importance of fitness in snooker becomes even more apparent. It is extremely difficult to cope with the pressures the game imposes on a player if he is not feeling clear-headed and 'on the ball'.

Alcohol consumption should also be

STAR TIP

I sometimes think there's no interim state between complacency and panic when you're playing snooker.
(Barry Hearn, after his client Steve Davis had lost 18–12 in the 1986 World Final)

KEY POINT

Temperament: if a player is to be successful in competition, it is crucial to control tension. Nerves often contribute to the defeat of a player more than the performance of his opponent.

kept to an absolute minimum when playing at whatever standard. Rather than calm the nerves, the consumption of large quantities of alcohol merely dulls the senses. This leads to judgement being impaired – and in a game which hangs on such small margin of error, this is calamitous. The vast majority of professionals, leading amateurs and even top local league players do not take alcohol before or during the course of a match.

PART 4

BILLIARDS

CHAPTER 14

THE RULES

The Rules

The game of billiards is played with three balls: two whites and a red. The game starts with the red on the spot (*see* Fig 150). Players spin a coin or 'string' for the choice of playing first, or for the choice of

12¾in

29in

11ft 8½in

11½in

5ft 10in

Fig 150   Playing dimensions of a billiards table.

the two white balls. One of these two balls has two small black spots and is referred to as 'spot', while the other is called 'plain'.

The first player may place his ball anywhere within the D for his first shot.

The first player must play the red with his first shot. If his white drives the red into a pocket (pot-red) or if his white enters a pocket after contacting the red (in-off red), he scores three points. If, on the other hand, he misses the red (a miss), his opponent scores two – the penalty for all misses and fouls.

When the first player fails to score, the second player places his ball anywhere within the D and may play at either the red or at his opponent's white, provided the latter is not in baulk (the area between the baulk line and the baulk cushion).

In addition to the methods of scoring outlined above, a player may drive his opponent's white into a pocket (pot-white), cause his own white to enter a pocket after striking his opponent's white (in-off white) or cause his own white to strike both the red and his opponent's white (cannon). Each of these scoring shots is valued at two points.

The game then proceeds with players taking alternate turns (or innings) until one of them reaches a pre-arranged points target (e.g. 100 or 1,000 points), although in most championships players play a variable number of two-hour sessions.

Each time a player scores an in-off, his ball is returned to him to place anywhere

within the D for his next shot. This is known as 'playing from hand'. When doing this, the player's own ball (cue-ball) must initially leave baulk before striking another ball.

Each time the red is potted, it is returned to its own spot. When this is occupied by another ball, it is placed on the pyramid spot. If a player pots the red from its spot twice in a row, it is then placed on the middle spot until it is potted again.

If a player pots his opponent's white, this remains in the pocket until it is his opponent's turn to play. On any occasion when a player fails to contact an object-ball (except when the striker is in hand and there is no ball out of baulk) his opponent, in addition to any penalty incurred, has the option of playing from the position left or having the balls spotted – red on its own spot, opponent's white on the middle spot and cue-ball in hand.

Players of an advanced standard have to watch for the 'fifteen hazards' rule (a 'hazard' is an archaic term for a pot or in-off). The rule limits a player to fifteen consecutive pots and/or in-offs. To continue his break, he must play a cannon at least once every sixteen shots. The referee 'warns' a player after ten hazards. A player is limited to seventy-five consecutive cannons but, since there are less than half a dozen players capable of maintaining such a lengthy sequence, this rule rarely needs to be applied.

Fig 151   If the red is potted off the left jaw of the pocket and the cue-ball is bounced a couple of inches from the right jaw, a half-ball in-off red will then be available when the red is re-spotted.

CHAPTER 15

IN-OFFS, POTS AND CANNONS

There are three methods (excluding penalties) by which a player scores at billiards, namely in-offs, pots and cannons.

In-Offs

The foundation of billiards is in-offs. Indeed, many players have reached amateur championship standard with a good command of in-offs and very little else. One advantage of the in-off game is that whenever you play from hand you can select the best position for the cue-ball, instead of being limited by the particular position of the balls.

Fig 152 (a), shot 1, shows the most basic and most valuable in-off in the game: the half-ball in-off into the middle pocket. The angle at which the cue-ball has to strike the red is an easy one for the eye to select, so, even for fairly inexperienced players, there should be little problem about the shot itself. The next step is to try to play the shot with just enough strength for the red to travel up the table, bounce off the cushion and return to almost the same place.

Using the game's most elementary shot, we are already involved in the essence of good billiards – positional play. Positional play is based on the habit of thinking one or two shots ahead, or even in groups of shots. Obviously, anything very complex is beyond the reach of the novice, but the standard 'in-off the red and bring it back' is well within anyone's capabilities with a little practice.

In the twenties the great Australian, George Gray, made many breaks of over 1,000 through this shot alone. This was as boring to watch as it was effective and led to a limitation of consecutive hazards to eliminate this monotonous element in the game. This limit has varied over the years and now stands at fifteen. After the fifteen hazard, a player must play a cannon to continue his break. However, the 'fifteenth limit' should not trouble novices until they have been playing for a year or two.

Fig 152 (b), shot 2, shows that the red has returned to almost, but not exactly, the same spot in which it stood for the previous shot. To preserve the same half-ball angle, it is necessary to move the cue-ball slightly further to the left than for the first shot.

So long as you can keep bringing the red back into the same area, you should continue to score quite easily, but there

Fig 152 (a)

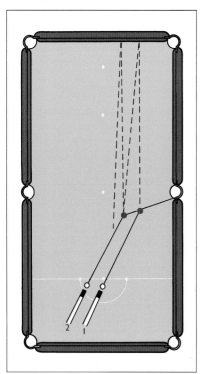

Fig 152 (b)

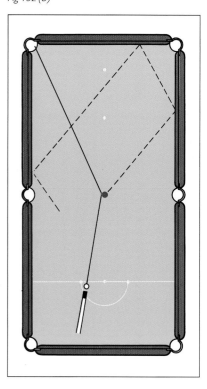

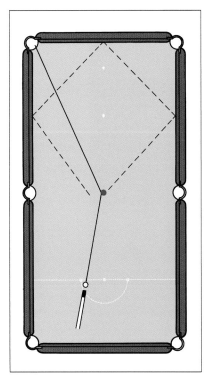

Fig 153

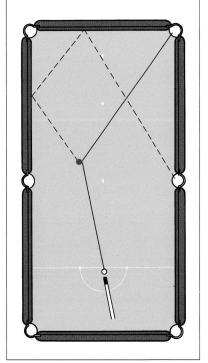

Fig 154

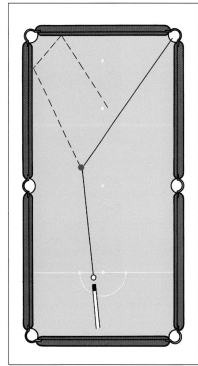

Fig 155

will be times when the red comes back either too far or not far enough. When the red does not come back far enough, you will have to play a long in-off, i.e. an in-off into one of the top pockets. This is harder than the standard middle pocket in-off, but it can be mastered through practice and recognition of the required angle to the extent that the shot is rarely missed. The first long in-off to master is with the red on the middle spot. Place the cue-ball a couple of inches inside the end spot, as shown in Fig 152 (a), and strike the red half-ball. Not only should the cue-ball disappear sweetly into the top pocket, but also the red should travel round the table off three cushions to offer a simple middle pocket in-off for your next shot.

For complete beginners, it is satisfying enough simply to execute the in-off successfully; however, you will soon realize that it is profitless to play 'one-shot-at-a-time' billiards.

If you are having difficulty with this shot, it may be that you are contacting the red

very slightly less than half-ball (sometimes referred to as a 'thin half-ball'), whereas, if anything, the red needs to be struck 'thick half-ball' (slightly more than half-ball). The reason for this can be seen from Fig 153, where the in-off has been played 'thin' half-ball. The red has sliced on to the right-hand side cushion, so that it strikes the left-hand side cushion almost opposite the pink spot, rather than about 9in (23cm) short of the middle pocket. On some occasions, the red will remain out of position for the next in-off, at best, will come only far enough for another long in-off or, instead of the much simpler in-off in the middle.

The only way to get the 'feel' of these shots is by constant practice. Some of the outstanding billiards players practise 'red ball play' – sequences of in-offs – by the hour. However, most good players find that shorter periods of practice, provided they are regular, pay ample dividends.

The in-off red from the centre spot can be used as a reference point for other in-

offs from that area. Start by placing the red a few inches to the right of the centre spot and try it to the left; also try placing it a little to the left and above the centre spot, and a little to the right and below the centre spot. As you vary the position you will begin to encounter certain problems. It may be that in some positions your thick half-ball shot is merely going to bring the red ball round into the middle pocket, giving you six points for the shot instead of three, but effectively ending your break.

Fig 154 shows what may happen if you try to bring the red round off three cushions, in the usual way. Figs 155 and 157 show two ways of avoiding this. In Fig 158, the in-off is played quite slowly, with just enough speed to bring the cue-ball off two cushions into the neighbourhood of the pink spot. In Fig 159, the in-off is played much more sharply as a thin half-ball – the very thing you were advised to avoid when playing the in-off red on the centre spot. However, a precise position alters general principles and proves that

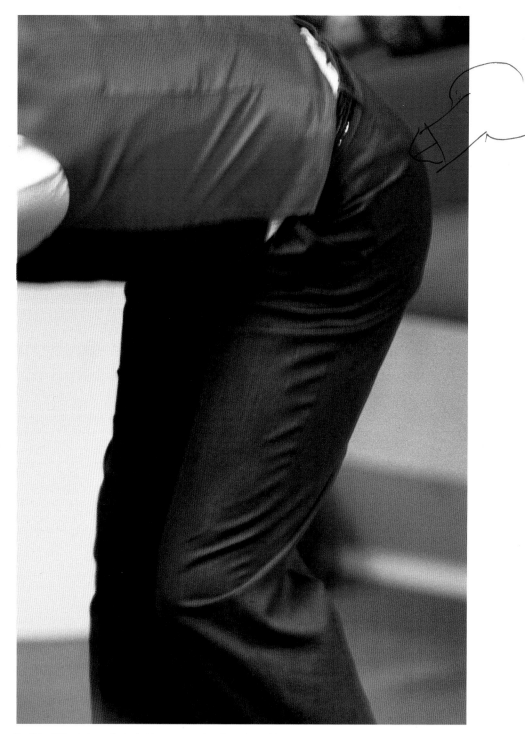

Fig 156 Billiards shares its basic grip, stance and cueing action with snooker.

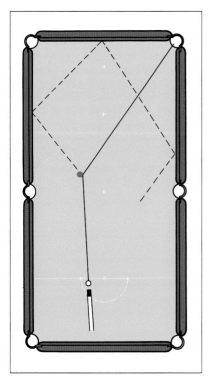

Fig 157

Fig 158

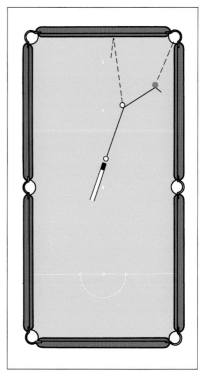

Fig 159

even a relatively straightforward branch of the game like red ball play has its pitfalls.

The position in which the red finished in Fig 155 leads us to another recurring type of in-off: the 'Y' in-off. A glance at Fig 160 (in the next chapter) shows the obvious derivation of this term.

Pots

Potting is not, of course, as important in billiards as it is in snooker, where it is impossible to get very far without being a fairly good potter. It is broadly true to say that in billiards it is more important not to miss easy pots than to have the ability to sink spectacular long-distance pots.

The art of billiards lies in controlling the balls in such a way that one easy shot leads to another. Ideally, a player tries to do this with snooker as well, but in snooker, he is very much more dependent on the precise position of the balls.

Some billiards players try to eliminate

potting from their game as much as possible, but there are certain types of po which recur constantly and must be mastered. The most notable of these is the pot-red from the spot. The great players of the past realized this to such an extent that big breaks were made purely by potting reds from the spot, just as George Gray made big breaks simply from going in-off in the middle pocket. These breaks, compiled by the so-called spot-stroke, led to a limitation of the number of consecutive pots which could be made from the spot. This limit has varied from time to time but now stands

---

KEY POINT

Practice: practice helps to hone a player's skills. If, as with most people, your time is limited, learn to make the most of these learning, improving and experimenting sessions.

---

at two. After two consecutive pot-reds from the spot, the red is placed on the centre spot, but is placed on its own spot when it is potted again. The fifteen hazards rule still applies, of course.

The best way to master potting the red off its spot is to place the cue-ball for a half-ball pot on the red and see how long you can keep a spot-stroke break going (see Fig 158).

Cannons

Just as the rules had to be changed to limit the long sequences of in-offs and pots, so they also had to be amended to eliminate long runs of cannons. Using the freak 'anchor cannon' (when the red and object-white were suspended on the upper and lower jaws of the top pocket) Tom Reed made one break of 499,135. This took him five and a half weeks and caused the anchor cannon to be outlawed. Much later, the Australian Walter Lindrum – by common consent the greatest billiards player in the history of the game – was the most notable of a group of players who mastered 'close cannons'. Close cannons are sometimes referred to as 'nursery cannons' because the three balls are 'nursed' gently along the cushion with a series of soft, delicate touches.

These sequences require very high degrees of skill but after a while are deadly dull to watch. Accordingly, a limit was set of thirty-five consecutive ball-to-ball cannons, which was raised to seventy-five

in 1971. This rule is likely to cause trouble to less than a dozen players in the world. For everybody else the cannon is a constructive linking shot rather than a prolonged means of scoring.

Fig 159 shows a typical constructive cannon from object-white to red, making contact gently with the red to send it over the top pocket, so that it can be potted with the next shot. It is difficult to go very far wrong with this shot, but it is worth noticing the final position of the object-white in this shot (i.e. within a few inches

if the red spot). This is an excellent place for the object-white to be, because, once the red has been potted, the two balls are obviously sufficiently close together for another cannon to help continue the break.

Good players are always looking for a chance to place the object-white near the spot, particularly with the shot shown in Fig 163 (in the next chapter), the standard 'drop cannon'. The idea here is to play from the inside of the object-white to the inside of the red in order to leave all three balls at the top of the table.

CHAPTER 16

AN INTRODUCTION TO BREAKBUILDING

The Opening Shot

Let us now take the opening of an imaginary game of billiards and see how the various strokes of the game weave into a pattern.

It used to be permissible to begin with a safety miss, but now the player playing the first shot *must* strike the red.

A 'double baulk', i.e. bringing both balls back into baulk so that your opponent cannot play a direct shot at either of them, is possible, but it is usually regarded, even by top players, as so risky (the penalty for

failure is usually leaving *both* balls *out* of baulk in a good scoring position) that they generally settle for the shot shown in Fig 160. Played perfectly, the cue-ball will finish tight on the side cushion, with the red near the baulk pocket diagonally opposite, as shown. In this position, it is exceedingly difficult to score or to prevent your opponent from scoring via the easy in-off red next shot, but we will assume that the shot is not quite so good and that there is a reasonable chance of a scoring stroke.

As Fig 161 shows, the shot to play is a cannon, but there is sometimes a problem

in that you cannot always play half-ball off the white, because the object-white will come off the side cushion and 'kiss' the cue-ball, thus ruining the shot. The solution is to spot further over towards the left-hand side of the D and to play more thinly, as shown in Fig 161.

The cue-ball may complete the cannon in a number of ways and it is as well to recognize that there is an element of chance in where the balls will finish, and whether your next shot will be easy or difficult. We will assume that the balls have run kindly to leave an easy in-off red, a

Fig 160

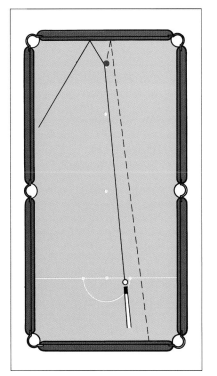

Fig 161

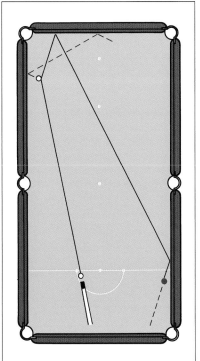

Fig 162

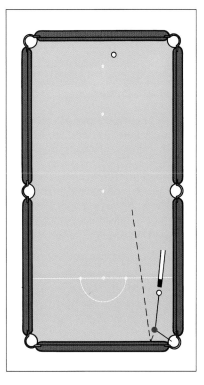

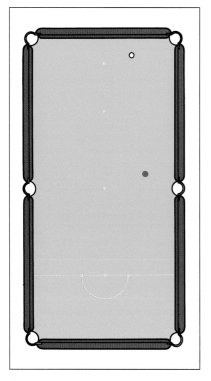

Fig 163

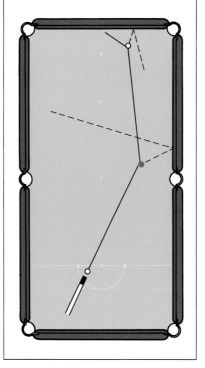

Fig 164

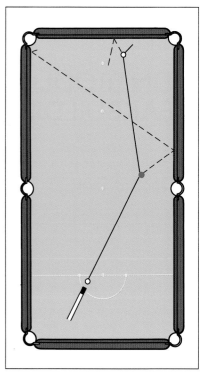

Fig 165

simple half-ball shot, which you will need to play at the right speed to bring the red out of baulk and leave an easy middle pocket in-off (see Fig 162).

Building a Break

The secret of successful billiards is to make one easy shot lead to another, utilizing such basic methods of scoring as the series of middle pocket in-offs to build up your breaks. These 'standard' shots which, with practice, you will integrate into your game so completely that you will rarely miss them, will not only keep you scoring but will also play you in, giving you the touch and confidence to play the more difficult strokes which may arise later.

Having gone in-off the red and played one or two in-offs in the middle pocket, the red may finish too short (see Fig 163) for another in-off, but be well placed for either a long in-off or a cannon. Since you must

play a cannon at least once every sixteen shots, and since in any case it is a mistake to rely too heavily on one scoring method (i.e. in-offs), the shot to play here is a cannon. However, it is not just a question of getting the cannon and taking a chance as to what position is left. Fig 164 shows what happens if the cannon is played thin (i.e. contacting the red less than half-ball). The red is sliced, as shown, on to the side cushion and finishes in the middle of the table, while the object-white goes down the table, leaving the cue-ball somewhere between them.

Sometimes, luck can be on your side and

KEY POINT

Playing conditions: learn to adapt to the idiosyncrasies of 'strange' tables. At club level, it is impossible to succeed with certain shots on certain tables. Poor tables are a great leveller.

---

you may have a scoring shot left, but even if you do, your general position will not be as good as if you had played the drop cannon correctly. The drop cannon, as its name implies, drops all three balls relatively close together at the top of the table. This can be done in several ways. In this particular position, a contact slightly thicker than half-ball is necessary on the red to double it towards the opposite corner pocket (see Fig 165).

This shot requires good judgement of angles, not only to make the cannon but also to make it in the correct way. The shot must also be played at a well-judged strength. It is no good, for instance, playing at speed merely to be sure of the cannon and sending the balls flying everywhere. Fig 165, however, shows one of the positions in which the balls may finish with a well-placed shot.

Another common position is shown in Fig 166 where, following the golden rule of keeping the game as simple as possible, the shot to play is the in-off, sending the

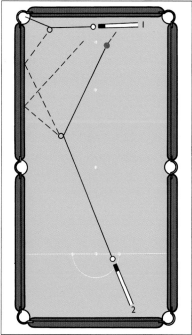

Fig 166

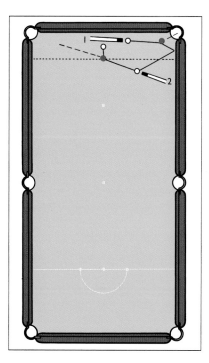

Fig 167

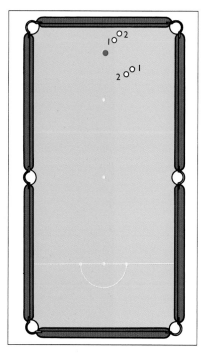

Fig 168

object-white up the table off the side cushion for another drop cannon (shot 1). The only pitfalls to avoid here are:

1.   Playing the shot too softly (in which case the red will finish under the cushion and prevent you playing an easy, natural drop cannon).
2.   Playing it too hard (which will again spoil your intended next shot, the drop cannon, though you will have the chance of a long in-off).

Because the half-ball in-off is such a fundamental stroke in billiards, players tend to find the half-ball angle an easy one to strike in cannon play too. The half-ball angle also makes for easy positional control, since a perfectly struck half-ball will mean that the speed of the cue-ball and object-ball after impact are identical. However, you will soon learn to use slightly thinner or, more often, slightly thicker than half-ball angles for drop cannons, often in conjunction with side.

In billiards certain basic shots recur. The certainty of control in these basic shots is one of the cornerstones of success, though one of the fascinations of the game is the innumerable different ways in which they may turn out.

Top of the Table

Fig 166, shot 2, shows that the object-white has finished very close to the spot, with the red easily pottable in the top pocket. This is the kind of position most top players strive for, since it enables them to build big breaks quickly and easily. This method, known as 'top of the table', can be utilized at any time when the red is on its spot and the object-white is behind the spot, i.e. in the 'box' marked by the dotted lines in Fig 167.

Even players of good league standard tend to subscribe to the myth that top of the table is too difficult for them; no sooner do they find themselves in a top-of-the-table position than they look for an in-off, in order to revert to scoring by in-offs and all-round play. This is nonsense, as it is just as valuable for moderate players to make thirty or forty points at the top of the table as it is for championship-class players to make 200 or 300.

Fig 167, shot 1, shows how the red is potted with the cue-ball crossing the dotted line to leave a cannon from red to white. Shot 2 shows the cue-ball contacting the red almost full on to send it towards the pocket and then cannoning so softly on the object-white that it hardly moves at all. (If the cue-ball remains on the dotted line or inside it, the cannon cannot be made without pushing the red away from a pottable position and knocking the object-white away from the spot).

The red can now be potted with a simple stun to bring the cue-ball back across the dotted line. (Again, if the cue-ball remains the other side of the dotted line, it is impossible to play a cannon sending the red towards the top pocket. The position left presents the opportunity to pot the red with a stun and to leave the cannon, i.e. virtually the same position as two shots previously.)

As you continue playing these pot-cannon sequences, the object-white goes further from the spot towards the

Fig 169 Bobbie Fodvari break-building.

cushion, often at an angle. As it does so (see Fig 168), you will need to remember that the cue-ball will have to be left at an increasingly sharp angle to the red in order to make your cannon. The one thing to avoid at all costs is getting a five-shot, i.e. the pot and cannon in the same shot, thus ruining your position and forcing you to break away from the top-of-the-table sequence. Sometimes, it may be necessary or advisable to bring the red off the side or top cushion so as to leave the pot-red (see Figs 170 and 171).

Fig 171 shows that it is also possible to make use of the top and side cushions of the pocket, playing the red on to the top cushion approximately 5 or 6in (12.7 or 13.2cm) from the pocket, so that it strikes the side cushion jaw and comes back into position for a pot. This is admittedly a fairly advanced form of top-of-the-table play but it is possible to make useful breaks at the top without it, particularly if at the first sign of danger you play an in-off in such a way as to enable you to regain top-of-the-table position (see Fig 172). It is easy to pot the red, but impossible to get the cue-ball round for the cannon, because the corner jaw is in the way. Therefore, play to leave the cue-ball on the top jaw of the corner pocket and to leave the half-ball in-off red from the spot. This will take the red up the table for either an in-off or a pot.

If, at this point, the red is positioned for a pot (see Fig 173), pot it and take the cue-ball up the table, as shown, into a top-of-the-table position. If the red falls short, play the in-off with the intention of bringing the red back slightly further in order to pot it. It is also possible to regain top-of-the-table position by means of a drop cannon, but since this means that the second object-ball must also be disturbed, this method is rather more chancy in terms of position than potting the red to *leave* the cannon. It is, in fact, the difference between having to control three balls rather than two.

When you have made a few points at the top of the table, the object-white may finish in the type of position shown in Fig 174. This is, incidentally, an excellent position in which to place the balls for

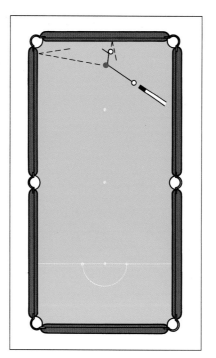

Fig 170

Fig 171

Fig 172

Fig 173

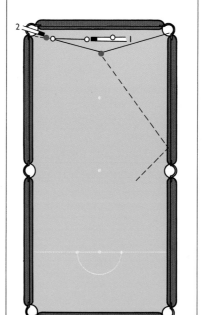

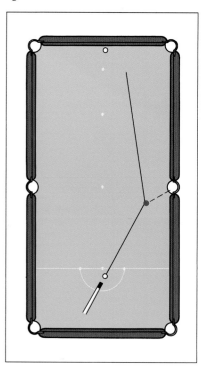

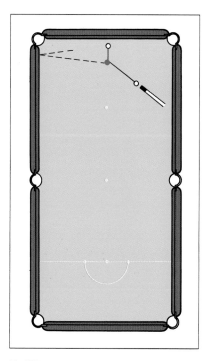

Fig 174

practice. If you can make forty or fifty
points regularly, it will mean that you
are developing the quality of touch
necessary for a successful top-of-the-table
player.

Postman's Knock

The first shot, as Fig 174 shows, is a
cannon from red to object-white, bringing
the red off the side cushion. In making full
contact on the object-white, the cue-ball
will ricochet back. You will hear two clicks
in quick succession: the usual one first (as
the cue-ball contacts the object-white) and
then the second (the object-white having
rebounded from the cushion) as the balls
meet again. This shot and this position are
known as the 'postman's knock' (*see*
Fig 175).

Having made the cannon, ensure, in
potting the red, that you get across the
imaginary dotted line, because you must
already be thinking of your next cannon.
So long as you finish almost anywhere
across the dotted line, you should have the

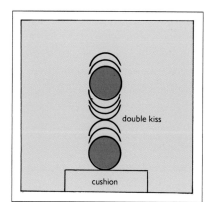

Fig 175

opportunity of another pot-red. Some
players indeed often take two pots – the
first with the red not on its spot, the
second with the red spotted – in getting
into position for the cannon. Fig 176
shows you have not left the cannon, but
can do so as you take the three points for
potting the red with a stun shot.

In general, though, too much potting

Fig 176

Fig 177

Fig 178

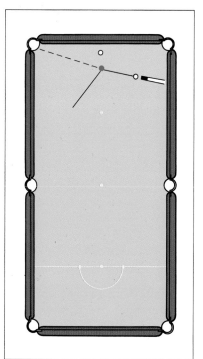

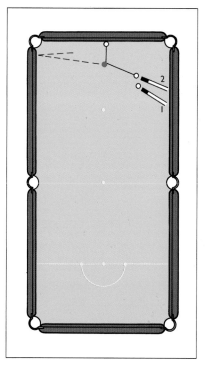

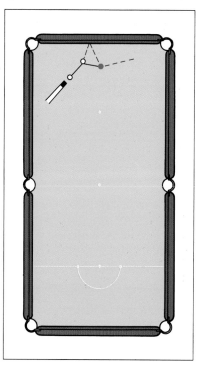

Fig 179   A tricky problem in snooker or billiards.

tends to upset the fluency, which is one of the secrets of good play at the top of the table.

Fig 177 shows that the cue-ball has not come quite far enough (i.e. to position 1) to play a repeat of the plain cannon full on the object-white, but the same shot can be achieved from position 2 by using strong right-hand side to throw the cue-ball wider. Manoeuvring the cue-ball into the right position for the cannon not only develops your judgement of strength, but will also be invaluable in snooker when operating round the black spot – which is vital in compiling big breaks.

Floating White

The 'floating white' technique is more complex, more varied and tends to be more satisfying to play, though it contains many traps. Figs 178, 180–182 illustrate some of the basic floating white moves.

Fig 178 shows that the object-white has strayed a few inches from the spot. You should, therefore, pot the red to leave a

half-ball cannon, as shown, to nudge the object-white on and off the top cushion back behind the spot – the ideal top-of-the-table position discussed earlier with Fig 181, shot 2.

Fig 180 shows another way of restoring the object-white to the ideal position. This shot is a little more delicate, because the half- to three-quarter ball contact on the red, as the cue-ball goes across it, requires more judgement and touch. If the contact on the red is too thick or too thin, it can spell disaster and the use of side can increase the possibility of a mistake. It is thus worth taking the trouble to position the cue-ball as precisely as you can when potting the red, in order to leave the plain-ball cannon.

Fig 181 shows the basic cannon off the top cushion, which is another way of keeping the object-white near the spot. Again, the groundwork is laid by the way the red is potted with a stun to leave a natural angle to ball-cushion-ball. A common fault is to make too thin a contact on the red, which tends to leave an

awkward thin cut-back pot-red for your next shot. Make sure that you push the red towards the side cushion, 5 or 6in (12.7in or 13.2cm) from the pocket, and complete the cannon gently by moving the object-white a couple of inches towards the spot. Whenever possible, play with a touch of right-hand side, so that the cue-ball can get right behind the red to make a cannon, which will nudge the object-white nearer the spot, rather than send it diagonally away from it.

Fig 182 shows a position which could lead to postman's knock by making a full-ball contact on the object-white to leave it dead on the top cushion. Instead, you can play half-ball to knock the object-white on and off the top cushion and leave it behind the spot.

There is an infinite number of variations of top of the table – one facet of the game which has the merit of being fun to practise by yourself. Even if you fail to conquer all its mysteries, it is a phase of the game which it is much better to know and play a little than not at all.

Fig 180

Fig 181

Fig 182

CHAPTER 17

OTHER AIDS TO BREAKBUILDING

Once you can play middle pocket and top pocket in-offs, can pot reasonably well from the spot and are conversant with screw, stun and side, you will gradually be able to add a number of useful shots to your game.

More Basic In-Offs

In-offs are the backbone of billiards, because, as we have seen, an in-off usually gives a player a wide margin of error in gaining position for his next shot. After an in-off, because the cue-ball may be spotted anywhere in the D, either or both object-balls need only be in the centre of the table (*see* Fig 183) for you to follow with an easy pot or in-off.

It is for this reason that top players, when they are struggling to keep a break going and when the red is on its spot, very often play to leave the cue-ball on or close to the four lines shown in Fig 184. These lines to the red all provide a basic half-ball in-off red, which is bound to leave the red well placed to continue the break, unless it is hit much too hard and put in baulk. Even when the cue-ball is not positioned precisely on these lines, the in-off is still feasible, within limits, if you use extra power, side or, occasionally, both.

If the cue-ball finishes on line A, the in-off can still be played half-ball if you use check (left-hand) side. The spin will not only narrow the angle at which the cue-ball leaves the red, but will also pull it towards the top cushion. Finally, the left-hand side will spin it off the far (i.e. side cushion) jaw of the pocket into the pocket itself.

When the cue-ball finishes on line B,

Fig 183

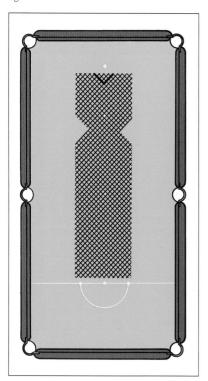

Fig 184

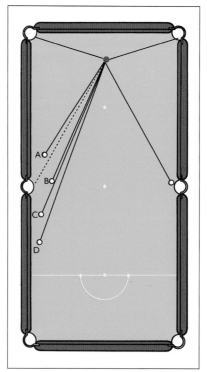

Fig 185

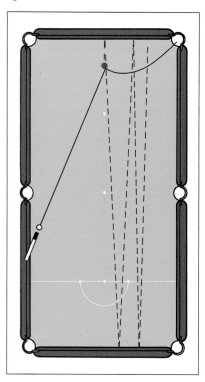

Fig 186 Playing a cannon – Norman Dagley, former World Professional Billiards Champion.

Fig 187

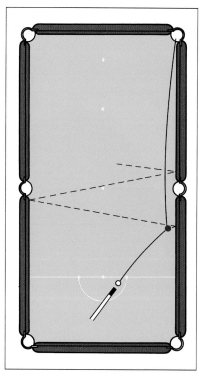

Fig 188

Fig 189

right-hand (running) side is needed to widen the angle at which the cue-ball leaves the object-ball, though the same widening of the angle can be achieved by playing the in-off more briskly and bringing the red in and out of baulk. The snag about the latter method (and indeed many forcing strokes) is that the red has a tendency to finish in baulk, as it is very difficult to control the speed of the red (and thus its final position) when any great power is used.

However, when the cue-ball finishes on line C, the angle is too wide for the in-off to be possible merely with the use of side, so a forcing stroke has to be used. The reason why this is known as a 'swing' in-off will be obvious from Fig 185. Whenever the cue-ball and the object-ball meet at any angle, except full-ball or almost full-ball, a 'throw' or 'bounce' occurs. In other words, instead of the cue-ball aiming away from the object-ball on a straight line (as most table Figs show for the sake of convenience), it describes a curve. The

more powerful the stroke, the more pronounced the curve. As soon as the cue-ball loses its initial speed, the curve disappears and the ball travels on a straight line. Thus, with forcing strokes which widen the angle, the shot has to be completed (in this case by the cue-ball entering the pocket) before the curve or swing has gone.

The wider the angle, the more power is required – bearing in mind also that, unless a solid half-ball contact is made, there will be insufficient curve or swing created to complete the shot successfully. With very wide swing in-offs (see Fig 184, line D) running (right-hand) side is also necessary to widen the throw from the red. However, it must be emphasized again that forcing swing in-offs can not only be missed more frequently than those played at medium speed, but also leave the ultimate position of the red largely to chance. Good players always play to leave the cue-ball on or very near line A and they generally regard having to play very

wide or very narrow in-offs as a sign that their positional play has gone wrong.

The other basic in-off is from the two corner pockets (see Fig 187). As the lines A, B and C show, this shot can be played without any side or with extreme side, depending on the precise position of the cue-ball. Another factor in this shot is the condition of the cloth. Side reacts more strongly on a fairly new cloth with a thick nap than it does on older cloth which has had more wear, and the amount of side used must be adjusted accordingly.

Jennies and Other In-Offs with Side

More difficult than the so-called 'cross in-offs' just discussed are the 'long jenny' and the 'short jenny'. The secret of both these shots lies in using plenty of check side.

The long jenny should be played briskly and, provided it is carrying enough side, the cue-ball can strike 3 or 4in (7 or 10cm)

Fig 190

Fig 191

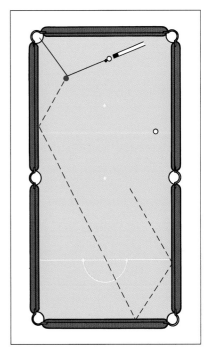

Fig 192

Fig 193

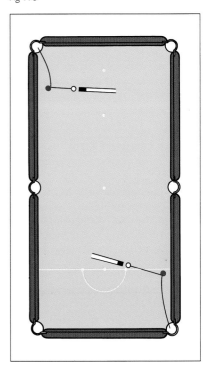

along the side cushion and still spin into the pocket off the top jaw (see Fig 188).

The short jenny calls for more precision and much less speed than the long jenny. As the cue-ball loses its momentum after striking the object-ball, the side should help it curl into the pocket, missing the near jaw and, still carrying plenty of spin, drop into the pocket off the far jaw (see Fig 189).

The run-through with side is another in-off which is invaluable in keeping a break going. When the object-ball is on a cushion (as shown in Fig 190 shot 1) the in-off, with practice, is quite simple. You should strike above centre with right-hand side (as always when using side, pushing the cue through the right-hand side of the ball and not brushing across it), contacting the red about three-quarter ball. The cue-ball will then run through, hugging the cushion because of the side it is carrying, and drop into the pocket.

The variation shown in Fig 190, shot 2, is slightly more difficult, because the object-ball is further away from the cushion. However, the principle of the

shot, i.e. extreme check (in this case, left-hand) side, is the same, even though the cue-ball, because of the different angle, will have to touch the cushion much nearer the pocket than in shot 1 in order to enter it.

Another extremely useful but more difficult run-through in-off is the one with running side shown in Fig 191. Here, right-hand side has to be used, making a nearly full contact on the object-white, with the intention of spinning the cue-ball into the pocket off the side cushion jaw.

There are many occasions when combinations of screw and side need to be used in in-offs. Fig 192, for instance, is a shot which recurs frequently. It is possible to play this shot half-ball with no side, but this will leave the red in baulk. It is much better to play thinner, with running (right-hand) side, to give the object-ball (the red) a wider angle off the cushion and thus bring it out of baulk. However, the nearer the object-ball gets to the side cushion, the more difficult it is to play in-offs with running side, because, if the cue-ball catches the top cushion jaw of the pocket,

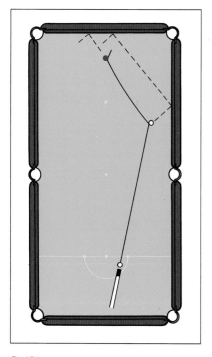

Fig 194

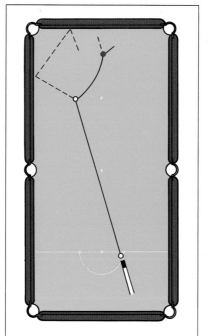

Fig 195

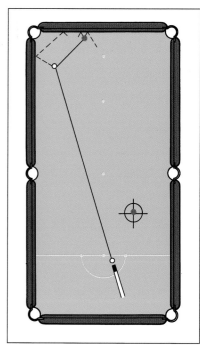

Fig 196

Fig 197

Fig 198

the right-hand side will keep it out of the pocket rather than help it in. In Fig 193, for example, the in-off is impossible with right-hand side but, with practice, it is quite easy with screw and left-hand side. Play quarter-ball with screw and left-hand side, and the cue-ball will hug the cushion because of the side it is carrying, and spin into the pocket.

Other Uses of Side

The uses of side, screw and stun in cannon play and potting are less easy to categorize.

As Fig 194 shows, running (left-hand) side can be used to widen the angle the cue-ball takes from the object-ball in order to complete a cannon, since, in this position, the plain-ball attempt at the cannon would result in the cue-ball going inside the red.

Fig 195 shows the use of check (left-hand) side to complete another drop cannon.

Side is, however, more often used by

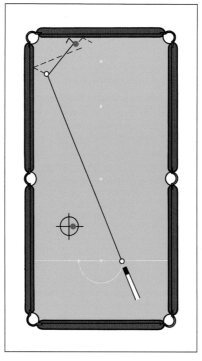

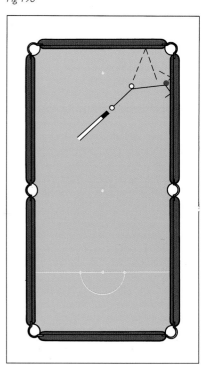

Fig 199   Norman Dagley potting the red.

players as a means of improving position. In Fig 196, for instance, you can place the cue-ball as indicated and play the straightforward ball-to-ball plain cannon. As the dotted lines show, this will leave the cue-ball between the two object-balls and awkwardly placed to continue your break. If you spot the cue-ball as in Fig 197, the difference is immediately apparent. Because the angle is wider, you will need strong right-hand side to complete the cannon, but the object-white will also be thrown wider and will bounce off the side cushion in such a way as to leave both object-balls nicely in front of the cue-ball.

The early part of this chapter was devoted to the ways in which players look for a basic half-ball in-off when they are in doubt as to the best way of keeping the break going.

The Gathering Shot

Another basic ploy is the 'gathering shot', so-called for reasons which are made obvious in Fig 198, on page 118. This particular shot is played strongly enough to bring the object-white back from the top cushion towards the red, as shown.

The precise position in which the balls will finish after a more difficult gathering shot – as when one of the object-balls has to be sent round the table off two or three cushions – may be more awkward to predict but, if you can develop enough touch to get all three balls to finish in a fairly small area, you will be most unlucky if you are not left with a reasonably easy way of continuing your break.

GENERAL GLOSSARY

Baulk   The area of the table between the baulk line and the bottom cushion.

Break   A sequence of scoring shots and the total points scored from one of them.

Check side   Spin which narrows the angle which the cue-ball takes from the cushion.

Cue-ball   The ball which is struck by the cue.

The 'D'   The semi-circle – radius 11½in (29cm) – which is inscribed on the baulk line and from which all strokes must be made when the striker is in hand. The cue-ball is in hand after it has either gone in-off or been forced off the table.

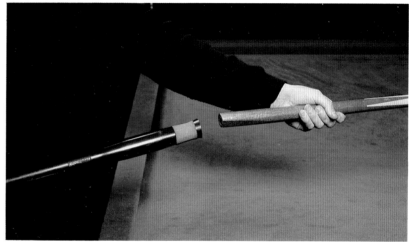

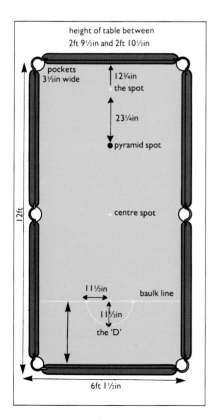

height of table between
2ft 9½in and 2ft 10½in

pockets
3½in wide

12¾in
the spot

23¼in

pyramid spot

12ft

centre spot

11½in   baulk line

11½in
the 'D'

6ft 1½in

Extension   A tubular device which is attached to the cue in order to lengthen it. By doing this, a player can reach awkwardly-placed shots and attempt them using his own tip.

Foul stroke   An illegal stroke, which results in penalty points being awarded to your opponent.

Frame   This is the term used for a single game. Matches are made up of an agreed number of frames.

Forcing shot   Any shot considerably above medium pace.

Full-ball shot   A contact in which the tip of the cue, the centre of the cue-ball and the centre of the object-ball form a straight line.

Half-ball shot   A contact in which half the cue-ball covers half the object-ball at the moment of impact.

In hand   The situation wherein a player, having scored an in-off (at billiards), can place the cue-ball by hand in the 'D' for his next shot.

In snooker, when one's opponent has gone in-off or forced the cue-ball off the

playing surface, the next shot is played from the 'D'.

In-off   When the cue-ball enters a pocket after contacting another ball. In snooker any shot which ends with the cue-ball in the pocket is described as an in-off, whether or not an object-ball is involved.

Jump shot   A foul shot, when the cue-ball jumps over the object-ball or any intervening ball.

Kiss   A second contact on the object-ball.

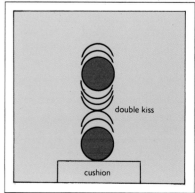

double kiss

cushion

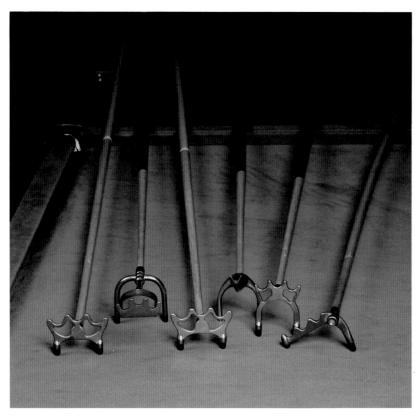

Natural angle   Any angle which the cue-ball may take after striking an object-ball at medium pace without a player imparting screw (back-spin) or side-spin.

Rest   This implement allows you to reach a difficult shot.

Running side   Spin which acts to widen the angle that the cue-ball takes from a cushion.

Safe position   When the balls are so situated that a scoring stroke is unlikely.

Safety shot   A shot from which a player does not hope to score but one where he is trying to place his opponent in an awkward position from where it will be difficult to score.

Screw   Back-spin applied to the cue-ball by striking it below its centre.

Side   Side-spin applied to the cue-ball by striking either its left- or right-hand side.

Spider   A rest with an elevated rest-head designed for awkward shots which require bridging over intervening balls.

Stun   A shot in which the cue-ball is stopped dead (dead-straight shot), or a shot in which the cue-ball is struck slightly below centre to widen the angle it takes from the object-ball (shot at an angle).

SNOOKER GLOSSARY

Angled If the cue-ball is obstructed by the jaws of a pocket in such a way that the player cannot see the object-ball, a player is said to be angled.

Break off The opening shot of a frame in which the striker plays at the unbroken triangle of reds.

Clear the table A sequence of shots in which the player pots all the balls left on the table.

Double A shot which involves an object-ball entering a pocket after striking one or more cushions.

Free ball If a player is snookered after a foul shot committed by his opponent, he may nominate any coloured ball as a red. If it is potted, he scores one point and then nominates a colour in the usual way. If all the reds have been potted, the free ball is nominated (valued at the same number of points as the lowest-value ball on the table) and the colours are then taken in sequence. For the purposes of this rule, a player is deemed to be snookered if both extremities of the object-ball cannot be directly hit (see page 18).

Maximum break A maximum break is a score of 147, compiled by potting the fifteen reds with fifteen blacks and then the colours in sequence.

Object-ball The ball 'on', the ball which the cue-ball is intended to hit.

Pot This is when the cue-ball is struck into the object-ball, sending the object-ball into the pocket (see page 51).

Plant A position in which the first object-ball is played on to the second object-ball in such a way as to make the second object-ball enter a pocket.

Set A position in which two object-balls are touching in such a way that the second ball is certain to be potted, however the first object-ball is struck.

Shot to nothing A position in which a player attempts to pot in such a way as to leave himself in position to continue the break if successful, but will leave the cue-

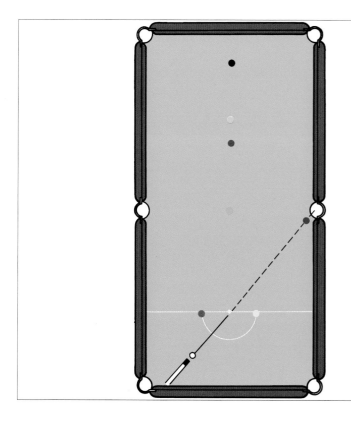

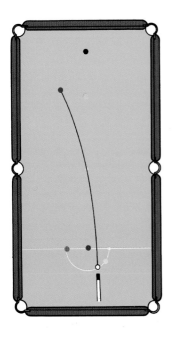

ball in a safe position for his opponent if unsuccessful.

Snooker   Any situation where the cue-ball cannot make direct contact with the object-ball as a result of intervening balls.

Snooker escapes   Tactical devices whereby the player makes contact with the object-ball, despite having been in a snookered position.

Stance   The balanced way in which the player holds himself so as to cue in a straight line. Each stance is individual, but the back leg should be braced, and the front leg bent. The weight is put on the front leg.

Swerve   This occurs when an extreme amount of side-spin is applied to the cue-ball in order to make its path curve. This type of shot, sometimes referred to as a 'masse' shot, is used for extricating oneself from a snooker (*see* page 89).

APPENDIX

Snooker and Billiards Tournaments

Established in 1916, the English Amateur Championship is the oldest event of its kind and a very difficult one to win.

It is organized by the Yorkshire-based Billiards and Snooker Control Council (B & SCC) along with an Under-19 and Under-16 championship, a pairs competition and for the past four years, an over-50 senior tournament known as the Grandmasters.

Entry forms for any or all of these can be obtained from:

B & SCC
92 Kirkstall Road
Leeds
Yorkshire
LS3 1LT

These national amateur championships are also part of snooker life in Scotland, Wales, Northern Ireland, Republic of Ireland and, as the game continues its expansion, most countries in the Commonwealth, Western Europe and the Far East.

All national associations, no matter how small, can send a maximum of two representatives to the annual International Billiards and Snooker Federation World Amateur Championship, which has been held in such varying locations as Bangalore, Sydney, Invercargill and Blackpool.

In Britain, the boom of the past fifteen years has led to a proliferation of open or pro-am tournaments which are usually staged over one day at a purpose-built centre with a large number of tables.

Most of these events are sponsored and added to the money raised from entry fees – averaging £10 – the prize fund is not insignificant.

Virtually every weekend throughout the year the 'have cue, will travel' brigade can compete somewhere in an open of this nature, the best example of which is the Everards Open at the Willie Thorne Snooker Centre, Leicester, in September where a first prize of £3,000 is at stake.

The same kind of financial incentive, and the fierce competition it attracts, can be found at the Pontins Spring and Autumn Festivals which take place at Prestatyn in May and October.

All these tournaments provide the training ground for tomorrow's professionals, whereas the network of local leagues allow less talented or ambitious cueists to have their weekly helping of competitive snooker.

Nearly every town of any size possesses its own league with anything up to ten divisions. Tournaments usually run from September to April.

Different leagues operate under differing formats, yet all assist a player in gaining often invaluable experience of match situations.

If you compete in a league for any length of time it is almost certain that you will be exposed to all manner of styles and approaches from the methodical, plain ball, safety-first plodder to the flamboyant, adventurous potter. This is likely to improve your game more than practice sessions with the same group of opponents, week in, week out.

Many players turn up religiously year in, year out on 'league night' and to them a particular league trophy can be as important as the world title to the likes of Stephen Hendry, Steve Davis or John Parrott.

INDEX

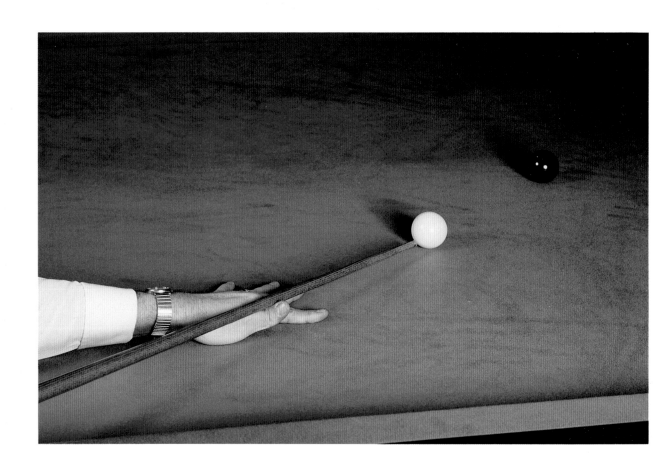